Praise for Soul Statements

"Corey's experience as a talented relationship coach, sexuality educator, vision quest guide and father provides a fresh perspective on finding healthy love. *Soul Statements* is an essential and practical guide for anyone who wants to communicate with greater empathy and emotional intelligence."

    -- **Judith Orloff, MD**, author of *The Empath's Survival Guide*

"In this warm and wise book, Corey Lyon Folsom teaches us to reach down inside and guide our lives with integrity and joy."

    -- **Catherine Auman, LMFT**, author of *Tantric Mating*

"*Soul Statements* plugs you into your own unique and essential voice, enhancing intimacy with yourself and all of life. This book will widen your capacity to channel your full expression!"

    -- **KamalaDevi McClure**, author of *Sex Shamans*

"This book touched my heart! In *Soul Statements*, we're encouraged to embody more of who we are through insightful journal prompts and thoughtful inquiry. I want to use the answers that arise to direct my life."

    -- **Lisa Tahir, LCSW**, author of *The Chiron Effect*

"Corey's writing in *Soul Statements* is so good – the Corey I know and love comes through his written word beautifully. This book is not to be missed – it and this man are a treasure."

-- **John Dupuy**, author of *Integral Recovery*

"*Soul Statements* is a rich and textured guide to caring for the soul. It has a delightfully positive emphasis on how inner work translates to manifesting a new experience in the world."

-- **Ronald A. Alexander, Ph.D.**, author of *Core Creativity*

"I felt uplifted and supported reading this useful book full of helpful tools and inspiration."

-- **Lisa Frechette**, author of *Transforming To Joy*

"Soul Statements offers a way to attune to the power of your own essence, the current of energy that is always streaming through you."

-- **Lorin Roche, Ph.D.**, author of *The Radiance Sutras*

SOUL STATEMENTS

A Love Coach's Guide to Successful Communication

COREY LYON FOLSOM

Core Relationship Coaching

SOUL STATEMENTS

Cover design and layout: Corey Lyon Folsom
Back cover photo: Michael Adams Headshots

Publisher: Core Relationship Coaching
First Printing, 2023

Print ISBN: 979-8-218-18885-6
Ebook ISBN: 979-8-218-18887-0

Cataloging-in-Publication Data for this title is available from the Library of Congress.

For my mother, Mary Folsom, a living example of positivity and

my most steadfast support,

and for my beloved Aurora, whose light illuminates my life.

Contents

WHAT THIS BOOK CAN DO FOR YOU

The cave you fear to enter holds the treasure you seek.
~ Joseph Campbell

If you long to become a more confident and graceful communicator, *Soul Statements* is for you. It offers a direct path to personal empowerment by teaching you how to effectively turn your inner voice into a constructive ally.

Each chapter has a wealth of simple, yet potent tools for relieving stress and upgrading your communication, mindfulness and connection. As a result, you can interact with family, friends and co-workers in a more caring and productive way.

Soul Statements will amplify your unique and essential voice, enhancing intimacy not only with yourself, but with all of life. Expect your capacity to love and care for yourself and others to expand as you powerfully connect to your wisdom and values.

This book is my personal invitation for you step into a deeper and freer version of who you were born to be. Imagine yourself stepping up and claiming more sovereignty and love. It is yours, if you want it.

We're here not to learn, but to remember what we already know, and then to experience it. ~ Neale Donald Walsh

If you crave more depth and ease, this book is for you. This book is for you if you are tired of repeating old patterns. It is a guide that will help you sustain meaningful and fulfilling relationships.

Greater intimacy and clarity of purpose can be found, not just longed for. This is not about becoming a new version of you, but re-remembering who you already are and living as that person. The journey within is a journey home.

To get the most out of this book, show up as if it is a coaching call and allow the questions to percolate in you. Expect your own revelations and answers to arise. You really are your own *head coach* as you grow in the ability to filter and choose your thoughts.

Soul Statements help you pay attention to internal alignment and this will lead you to be increasingly present to life. Your internal compass is never off, although your viewing of it may get fuzzy. The ultimate goal of *Soul Statements* is to help you readily access a state where you can hear your own signal. Enjoy being you and remember, direction is more important than speed.

This book is not meant to be read like a novel. Too much information becomes white noise and is generally not the answer to getting unstuck. When you pause and answer the prompts as you encounter them you can best integrate the material and make the teaching your own. This way, you'll quickly learn what helps you thrive in the real world.

Who looks outside dreams, who looks inside awakens.
~ Carl Gustav Jung

Note: I employ the terms 'feminine' and 'masculine' while understanding that a person can be embodying or emphasizing more of one or another irrespective of their foremost gender identity. 'Masculine' qualities generally being direction and focus and 'feminine' qualities generally being connectedness and flow, for example.

As a young man I didn't speak up for my needs and was too shy to talk to women. I shrank from my exuberance and certainty. My early intimate relationships were defined by poor patterns and I found myself in a sexless marriage made more difficult by my less-than-optimal relationship skills.

There have been big shakeups along the way. Three divorces. My children living in another state. An ocean surfing accident. A horse-riding fall. A cancer diagnosis. Each of these events informed my priorities and perspective. A shining life had eluded my grasp for too long. I had to decide that my past and my conditions would no longer define me.

There were innumerable acts of grace along the way and each breakdown eventually became a breakthrough. I hired a life coach as part of my deep study into understanding masculine-feminine dynamics. I chose this person as getting to where I wanted to be, in terms of intimate relationship, was territory that he'd already traversed.

I participated in numerous personal development courses in addition to being in extended love relationships with esteemed dakinis (female tantric practitioners). I consider myself to be incredibly fortunate, since formal training in the art of sacred loving is rare.

My shortcomings, failings and mistakes may have temporarily deflated me, but ultimately fueled me. As I became more willing to tell the truth to myself, my life improved. As I claimed my place in the world, greater inner and outer ease was the result. When I stopped practicing what wasn't really me, everything changed. I went from needing desperately to work on myself to coaching dynamic people from all over the world.

The greatest teacher is inside each one of us. This teacher is not a separate entity from you. There is no mysterious code in order to communicate with this teacher. This teacher is who you are. This teacher knows why you are. This teacher shows up as your inner knowing. But, we each must make some quiet space to listen to this teacher's message.

Be in love with your life. ~ Jack Kerouac

If your life is dispiriting in some areas, what is in the way of claiming a better experience? What will it cost you to remain where you are? Where will you be in 5 or 10 years if your direction doesn't shift now? What would your loved ones miss out on if you don't express your highest gifts? Did you show up here with dreams only to not live into them? I think not.

This book, *Soul Statements*, offers:

Tools for more successful communication.

Ways to claim your value, your voice and your place
in this world.

Simple practices to deepen your intimate relationships.

A guide to increased presence and love.

Resources to live as a more empowered version of you.

This is a time of global and individual searching and re-setting. We must accept and embrace our failings and our grace. The world needs your unique contribution. Loss is all around us: forests, coral reefs, civility, tolerance... However, all is not yet lost. We are at the edge of a precipice and the question is, '*Will we step up, both collectively and individually?*'.

This book is for you if you have a "*Yes*" to the following:

I am ready to access the deeper me.

I desire to be a better communicator.

I want to live as the person I was born to be.

I deserve increased ease in my relationships.

I'm honored to be your ally. Jump into the deep with me and see what treasures are there for you. Your depth is calling. Right now. What you do now will shape your destiny. If you've found this book, you may very well be ready.

Yes, I _________________________________ *am ready.*
(*write your name here*)

The Moment My Life Changed

I was sitting with 90 of my peers in a weekend workshop that was about to end. I felt a burning desire to finally confront my deep-seated fear of embarrassment. This was my very last possible moment to speak up as the facilitator took back the microphone from the final speaker.

I felt freedom tugging at my heart, yet fear sat like a heavy anchor in my chest. My desire to be free pushed harder. I heard the familiar small voice in me say, "later". I knew it was do or die right now. I could speak up or continue living a small life and forever second-guess what could have been.

I rose to my feet, walked onto the stage and accepted the microphone. I briefly shared my story of the way fear had controlled my life. I stood there raw, naked, honest and open and let myself be seen. My paradigm of who I could be shifted forever in that moment. What kind of life would I be living now if I hadn't confronted that pernicious layer of shame? What if fear-based decisions were still prevailing in my head? I would be living a smaller life.

We aren't broken, simply unfinished. ~ Amanda Gorman

2

SOUL STATEMENTS

*You don't need techniques as much as to just remember
who you are.* ~ Tony Robbins

A typical affirmation is a declaration to help a person emotionally inhabit a desired experience. Even though stated in present tense, it is feeling into what you wish to become or have. Affirmations are very useful, but a Soul Statement is not an ordinary affirmation. A Soul Statement is a simple and profound reminder of what is already true, which creates greater coherence between your surface thinking and your deep knowing.

Soul Statement Example
Wisdom is at my center.

A Soul Statement is a present-time declaration about the unchanging nature of your soul. A Soul Statement is not a way to 'fake it until you make it'. You're not attempting to lie to your brain. It is a tool to grab hold of what is unchanging about you and let your true essence guide your next thought and action.

Declaring a Soul Statement is a way to quickly drop down beneath surface thinking and embody a more grounded state. A Soul Statement tunes your thoughts to be more in line with what's most right about you and what you value.

This upgraded thinking helps illuminate which of your current desires are in line with your soul's purpose. The appropriate next action for you will now be more obvious.

We each have a deep place within that underlies personality, behavior and circumstance. This is where your certainty and purpose resides. Awareness of certainty and purpose naturally fades as mundane tasks occupy one's attention.

A Soul Statement is a tool to re-anchor you in a moment to what matters most. A Soul Statement is stand for the truth of who you are. It's a brief touching of your depth. Your personal Soul Statement can be a reminder of your innate sovereignty.

Soul Statement Examples
In my center, I belong.
I am held in love.

Many people experience their depth as a feeling of arriving at their center place. This is where inner knowing lives. You'll feel more solid and sure when you're in touch with the solid and sure place within you. A Soul Statement is like a lifeline back to the ship when you find yourself overboard in a choppy sea of events.

My coaching clients consistently find this to be an effective method to quickly return to alignment, in real time, with who they really are. When you are aligned in this way, you'll naturally live more congruently as #TheRealYou.

Making Your First Soul Statement

Don't get stuck on picking the perfect Soul Statement. Your Soul Statement at this time can be the first of many. Your preferred Soul Statement will certainly evolve and change. To create a personal Soul Statement, begin with the following exercise.

Personal Journaling Exercise

The qualities I love and treasure about myself are...
What's true about me (deep down) is...
Feel the emotion associated with this part of your essence.
The single most powerful true statement about who I am is...

Declare your newly-chosen Soul Statement silently or aloud along with feeling a relevant emotional charge. Bask in the clarity this brings. Your Soul Statement is now a homing device, a mnemonic, a lodestone and internal compass pointer.

Much like a bicycle wheel is trued by making many small adjustments, you can be increasingly aligned with your center by generating a Soul Statement as often as needed. Allow this increased clarity to inform your feeling, thinking, posture and behavior.

Soul Statement Examples

I am a treasure.
My heart is loving and strong.
Earth energy is at my core.

Your Soul Statement is a tool that gets sharper with use! Use it as a personal truth-calibration to get yourself back on track quickly with minimal drama and anchor you into greater internal calm. Note: The goal is not stay on top of things, but to get to the bottom of you.

Basic Soul Statement formula
Feel your true essence and declare a relevant Soul Statement silently or aloud.
Emotionally anchor into the truth of this Soul Statement.
Make your next action congruent with your Soul Statement.

Use your Soul Statement as a self-inspiration or an effective response when your mind repeats unhelpful phrasing. Allow the knowing underneath the Soul Statement to wash through your whole body and light up your cells.

The greatest value is when you can feel the truth of your declaration in your body. The Soul Statement is a tactic to achieve a soul-level knowing in your conscious awareness.

Soul Statement Questions
A powerful Soul Statement for me right now is...
What's a small step I can take now to align with this Soul Statement?

Find Your Own Querencia
In a bullfighting arena, the *querencia* refers to the secure space that the bull finds for itself. This is the location where he feels most comfortable and empowered. This is where the bull will return to in order to collect his energy.

A querencia is a place the bull naturally wants to go to in the ring, a preferred locality... It is a place which develops in the course of the fight where the bull makes his home. It does not usually show at once, but develops in his brain as the fight goes on... In his querencia he is inestimably more dangerous and almost impossible to kill. ~ Ernest Hemmingway

Your most powerful Soul Statement can bring you to your own *querencia*. That is the secure knowing place, which you return to in order to collect yourself. This place inside is where you may acknowledge distress and make it all alright. A Soul Statement can let you access the strength of your character and allow this knowing to inform your next action (or non-action).

A Soul Statement is a condensed message of knowingness from the deep you to the surface you. Your deep knowing is always available, but you have to intentionally tap into it. The world offers limitless distraction. You must intentionally choose to turn down the volume on the external world.

Start off each morning with a Soul Statement and declare it as needed throughout the day. Use a Soul Statement to re-affirm your value and your values on the go. Doing the work early and often does an elegant emotional ninja make.

Soul Statement Examples (to begin the day)
There is a well of contentment inside me.
There is ease at my center.
Love sustains me.

Your brain is a great survival tool, but is not the most intelligent part of you. **Question thoughts that bring you down and trust answers that arise from your center.** Make the voice in your head a personal coach and script how you want to speak to yourself in advance.

Have a Soul Statement ready for when you're triggered to more quickly return to ease. Let the ease that you achieve accompany you into a more empowered response or action.

The brain responds to repetition. Just as a craftsman gathers tools before going to the jobsite, you can build a toolkit to counter unhelpful thinking and of forgetting who and what you are. Repeat your personal Soul Statement and feel the associated feeling as often as you wish to anchor to the true you.

Personal Journaling Exercise
How often could I benefit from brief contact with my center?

Counteract Anxiety
One of my coaching clients would experience extreme anxiety in social settings. His life structure put him in crowded situations often and he would be emotionally paralyzed in the moment and then remain distraught for days after. He'd go to a place of feeling *"less than"* and would repeat a story of being snubbed, looked down upon and judged negatively by others. His anxiety was not making him better or giving him a better experience.

When he learned to give his brain a different message at those times of self-doubt by using a Soul Statement everything changed for him. With conviction, he said, *"I am enough"*, and *"These people are lucky to meet me."* He really felt the emotion of this personal truth. This was a whole-being emotional posture adjustment for him.

Amazingly, where once he was essentially invisible and ignored, he soon found people searching him out to talk and connect. This simple and potent shift of attitude literally changed his life overnight.

We've all spent a good portion of life essentially swimming on the surface of the deep lake of our true essence. When you contact and claim your true nature, you're freed from pretense and confusion. Any habit of lying about what you are capable of falls away. Harder choices become less difficult.

The doing may still be challenging, but the choice to align with values and integrity is less of a choice and more of a must. By applying Soul Statements, a more integrated you can become an increasingly more natural state. It is a beautiful moment when you can say, *"This is me. I commit to living true to myself."*

Your soul lives below story and personality. When you find the quiet at your center, you'll find clarity. One dependable way to discover what is important and true is by becoming still and allowing emotions to bubble up.

Since emotions are not always easy to feel, you must be willing to become uncomfortable at times. Allow feelings to just be present without pushing them back down. If need be, pause to offer empathy to yourself. If you honor strong emotions, you will find that they carry important soul-messages.

In the historic Native American Great Plains warrior tradition, there were Sash-Wearer societies (sometimes referred to as Dog Soldiers). The Ponca called one of theirs the, *Make No Flight ~ Not Afraid to Die Society.*

A sash-wearer was universally respected because, in a battle, he would place himself between opposing forces and pin the end of his sash into the ground with a lance. There he would stay and fight, until he was either killed by an enemy or released by another society member.

When you put a virtual stake in the ground, it is good to know what ground you're on. In his poignant song, *Crazy Horse*, John Trudell sings, *"Too many people standing the wrong ground."* The process of creating a Soul Statement helps one choose the right ground on which to stand.

Your Soul Statement is a Go-To thought that you give your brain a good message during a time of distress or uncertainty. A Soul Statement returns you to what matters. Standing in your center allows you to rotate around your own axis. In order to let the world know who you are and what you stand for, you must first know this for yourself.

A Soul Statement can be your own virtual Dog Soldier sash to anchor into your most steadfast self. In the words of John Cougar Mellencamp, *"If you don't stand for something, you'll fall for anything."* Discover what you stand for and the winds of life will feel more like breezes more of the time.

Personal Journaling Exercise
Where have I put a metaphorical stake in the ground?
Am I standing on the right ground?
Where have I moved my virtual line in the sand?
How will I act differently in the future?

It is a powerful act to claim your belonging in this world. When you do this, fear dissolves into the nothingness that it always was. In middle school, fear of a bully held me back from standing up for myself.

He had me cowed through my aversion to being hit, kicked and embarrassed. It took most of a school year for me to finally say, *"I'm not listening to you anymore."* When I spoke those words, he immediately lost interest in me. I never interacted with him again.

With the benefit of time, I now wonder if my guardian angel sent this bully to me so that I could have an early demonstration of a situation working out alright when I take a stand for Corey. This may be an example of life working in one's favor, even when it doesn't seem like it at the time.

Personal Journaling Exercise
When and how do I make myself small?
Do I avoid difficult conversations because the negative energy
is "just not worth it"?
Do I hedge when saying, "No" would support my values?

What would happen if I change focus to emphasize my
strength and resiliency?
What action could I take to reclaim my voice and power?

For years, I let fears inform my important decisions. I shied away
from people and choices that would require more of me - more
intimacy, more energy, more risk. My intimate partners were often
looking forward to the day that my full presence would shine forth.
Mostly, they just waited. I was lost in a thicket of indecision and an
inability to imagine a life of wide contribution and optionality.

I never struggled with substance abuse, but found it incredibly
helpful to work through the Twelve Steps of Alcoholics Anonymous
(AA), whereby I replaced the word *alcohol* with the word *fear*.

Working the amazing and difficult AA Twelve-Step process was
foundational in preparing me for a greater life than I had previously
been able to envision. I often reference the AA principles and dic-
tums to this day. (Reference: Alcoholics Anonymous: The Big Book;
Fourth edition, 2002)

AA Step One (as I personally worked it)
I admitted I am powerless over fear, that my life had
become unmanageable.

Soul Statement Examples
My soul-knowing is more powerful than my fear.
My soul informs me.
My heart is a trusted guide.

*Some years ago, I was frustrated and tired of living in a low-energy
state. My mojo was nowhere to be found. Unable to connect to my juice, I
became willing to risk embarrassment (my biggest fear). So, I brought my
angst to a small group of trusted friends.*

I surrendered to intense waves of emotional pain. I let myself wallow in feeling disconnected and impotent. I cried and raged. I stomped the floor. I knelt and pounded a pillow. At one point I fell forward and accidentally knocked my forehead on the floor. I was not holding back. All that I could feel was sorrow and loss.

My companions held a secure, loving field as I agonized and wept. They did not try to fix me or comfort me. Then, one wise elder spoke. He said that the volcanic magma energy that is deep within the Earth is also within me. He suggested that I imagine having magma in my belly.

I did so and right away there was a heat burning inside me. My fear evaporated like a fog bank under a warm sun. I felt sure power in my center. I knew then that strong emotions can be converted to power when embraced and well-directed. I understood that my fearlessness was key to a greater experience of life.

My agony had lifted. There was nothing more to strive and yearn for. The search was over. I felt grounded, complete and powerful. I needed no external confirmation of any kind. This re-ignition of my inner fire was a reclaiming of my essence and my strength. My life was very different from that time forward.

In the previous story, I had to be willing to risk losing the respect of my companions. Embracing the purity of my uncomfortable emotions, no matter who was watching, enabled me to have an important breakthrough.

Having courage actually requires fear, as it is letting your heart override your fear. The word courage comes from the French, *couer*, which means heart. So, the literal translation of courage is, *heartfulness*.

Re-igniting my inner fire was incredibly liberating and powerful. The fire in my belly was now a protective force for my heart. The heart is sometimes referred to as the *inner beloved*. A time when you feel alone and abandoned can be an opportunity to go deeper.

When I made contact with my *inner beloved*, I committed to never knowingly abandoning him again.

I consistently work to honor and sustain the real Corey now that I've found him. Fear lives in the absence of understanding. Just as light banishes darkness, inner illumination brings peace and serenity. It is also helpful to remember that **fear can be real without being true**. In other words, an emotion is occurring irrespective of that emotion being based in a true version of events.

Soul Statement Examples

I have a beloved that dwells within.
When I confront my fear, it diminishes.
There is a fire deep in my core.

Physiology

Physiology contributes significantly to the way we feel. When using a Soul Statement, some people sense tingling skin. Other people will have a neutral knowing and/or feel more solidly anchored into their body. You may feel these changes and more at different times.

Including a congruent physical posture magnifies the impact of a Soul Statement. Making a shift in physical posture is a way to change one's emotional state. I'll commonly straighten my spine, slightly raise my diaphragm and add a power gesture to a Soul Statement as a way of involving my neurology.

A power gesture is anything you want it to be. A fist pump is one example of a power gesture. Some people like to place a hand over their heart. Still others will simply nod their head or stand a little straighter. I use all of these at different times.

A physical posture shift is a supporting message to your brain that anchors you to a power state. Adjusting your posture has an immediate effect on how you feel. It's hard to be super-happy while your back is curled and shoulders drooping. It's challenging to feel depressed when doing jumping jacks. Adopt a coherent posture as an integral part of your Soul Statement practice to up-level your results.

Soul Statement Practice

Declare a Soul Statement while adopting a matching
body posture.
Feel the deeper impact this has. Do it again. Claim it
as your own!

Spiritual Pushups

It is useful to remind oneself how much grace underlies and infuses life. I call feeling grateful a *"spiritual pushup"*. Feeling even a bit of gratitude reliably provides me with an emotional posture adjustment. It's hard to be grumpy and grateful at the same time! Soul Statements that increase gratitude are also a form of *spiritual pushup.*

Take the next opportunity to counteract a deflated state and anchor to a more solid and optimistic attitude by dropping down and giving yourself 10 gratitudes. Add a Soul Statement to cap it off and go forward into your day from this improved state.

Personal Journaling Exercise (spiritual pushups)

Make a list of 20 things that you're grateful for.
Do this first thing every morning for a month.

Power State Meditation

Sit in a comfortable position and close your eyes. Roll your shoulders, stretch, breath, sigh or yawn as needed to create more ease.

Breathe naturally without effort. Imagine that you have grounding cord (as a column of golden light, a tree root or whatever you prefer) that is anchored from your hips deep into the Earth. Notice how gravity holds you where you sit.

Let this grounding cord exert a slight energetic pull as you begin to envision a grounded power state. Inhabit the felt sense, posture and emotion of this state. Feel this grounded version of you without any pressure to act. Keep feeling into your body. There is no rush.

Notice where you feel more open in your body. Allow that openness to expand into a wider area as you breathe. Practice feeling deeper ...and deeper. Be still and feel. Remain in this grounded and open state as long as you wish.

Intentionally claim this open and grounded feeling as something which you own. Realize that your future interactions can happen while you inhabit this powerful place.

Returning to Center

Life is a process of returning to one's centerline again and again and so it shall always be. The pain of drifting off center is all too familiar for most of us. Being in a stressed-out state is not attractive or sexy. Juggling many priorities and being over-busy engenders rushing and distress.

Living exclusively from surface thoughts results in desires being mistaken for values. Success is not about completely avoiding mistakes, but rather in growing the ability to course-correct and move forward in a good direction.

In my twenties I had the perfect job for taking me away from groundedness. My role was to troubleshoot tough problems that small, nomadic groups were having in a wilderness-based substance recovery program. My immediate supervisor worked out of another state and I handled emergencies large and small all day, every day.

I worked every waking hour for up to twenty-nine days a month. I got a lot of physical exercise, mental challenge and emotional satisfaction, but my daily self-care was spotty at best. By the end, my body weight was 112 pounds. Practically no one is as unbalanced to the degree I was then, although most of us can relate to being *off* for periods of time.

Get Better

One of my sons was a professional MMA fighter. During practice, he had to wrestle with whomever his coach assigned to him on a given day. When he got really worked over by a sparring partner, his attitude was that every experience is an opportunity to improve. I love the attitude of, *'this difficulty is making me better'*. This is one reason why he is my hero.

Soul Statement Example

I so got this.

Jocko Willink speaks about the habit he developed of saying "good" to anything that his superiors or charges in the military brought to him. If this was notice of a screw-up, that became an opportunity to learn how to avoid repeating a particular mistake. In intimate relationship and in all of life, the attitude and practice of making everything an opportunity to improve is a powerful way to ratchet up one's overall performance.

In the face of difficulty or setback, there are three choices:

1. Give up
2. Get better
3. Pause and re-evaluate

When you shift your attention from circumstance to unchanging truth about yourself with a Soul Statement, you shift into a more potent version of you. Feeling the deeper you is a way of filling up your emotional and spiritual well.

From this resourced state, you're better able to create healthy boundaries regarding what you're capable of in the moment. When you remember what is most important, you can communicate with fairness and compassion more readily.

Chapter Summary

A Soul Statement brings you into your clarity, power and presence in real time. Your body is wise and its responsiveness will let you know when you're moving in the right direction (and when you're not). Increased knowledge certainly has great benefit and applied knowledge is what matters most.

Apply a Soul Statement, with as much emotion as you can bring, as needed with the recognition that your attitude is aligning you with your next right action and your destiny.

Incorporate congruent physiology. Keep doing your *spiritual pushups* and choosing the right ground.

What if all is forgiven and standing for honor, integrity and serving a greater good is an important enough achievement? I believe that it is.

In the next chapter we'll go deeper into inner stillness and explore your primary relationship commitment, along with self-negotiation, building personal presence and honoring body cues.

If you are moved to, tag me in a social media post making a Soul Statement, with the hashtags #soulstatement #livetrue #innerfire

3

BE PRESENT TO WIN

*What lies behind us and what lies before us are small matters
compared to what lies within us.* ~ Ralph Waldo Emerson

If it were easy to push past fear then we would all be living like royalty. Sure knowing is at your center. The lock and key to a bigger expression is hidden there. Fear of depth is just fear. Bigger is possible. A bigger version of you is a gift to yourself and to the world. This bigger you cannot be pulled forward from the past. It can only be felt and claimed in present time.

Soul Statement Example
There is a lot right with me.

A Soul Statement is a way to re-capture the feeling of you during the bustle of everyday life. Cultivating clarity and presence is increasing one's personal power. However, you must be present to win.

*"Our minds, however, are born wanderers — perpetual refugees
from presence, perpetually paying for their flight with loneliness.
We go on forgetting that we are not only embodied creatures,
but embodied in the body of the world; we go on forgetting that
the here and now... is our only refuge from the existential loneliness
that is the price of being alive."* ~ Barry Lopez

A bigger you lives, it lives in your depth. A Soul Statement brings you more into your power and presence in real time. Aligning values, purpose and action is a winning formula. Honesty with self is power.

Bring forth your curiosity, desire, doubt and courage. This type of honesty includes being willing to hear information that will make it more difficult to live out of sync with the reason that you're on the planet.

On my deathbed or shortly thereafter I imagine I'll be remembering the depth of love, intimacy, openness and the contributions I made. So, it stands to reason that everything else is of lesser importance.

Soul Statement Examples
I remember who I am.
All is well.

In my coaching practice, I help people connect to the wisdom of their body and to slow down enough to hear inner messages. The present moment is a moving target. Time goes so fast. Balance the momentum of the world with inner stillness.

You can access your inner truth anytime you wish. You just have to stop listening to the noise of everything else. Your body, and the moment, is where truth lives. Find the moment and you've arrived where you need to be.

Soul Statement Examples

My body is wise and knows exactly what I need.
There is a place at my center where I can tune out
everything that is not me.

Inner Stillness Saved Me

I shouldn't have survived the mile-wide Kahiltna Glacier crossing. We were a group of three persons who were traveling fast to avoid being caught on the ice field in the developing twilight and thickening ground fog. I had stopped to rest and now my two companions were out of earshot. I yelled for them to help orient me, but they'd been swallowed up in the vast and wild Alaskan landscape and my voice was lost in the ground fog.

I walked on, but was soon stopped by a blue-black crack in the ice that was 35-feet across and 150-feet deep. I searched for a ¼ mile both left and right, but the only way across the chasm was a 2-foot wide slick-smooth ice bridge that started about thirty inches below the glacier rim.

I put crampons on my boots for my very first time, hoping the buckles were done right. The step down was tricky, but doable by going slowly. However, once I was standing on the ice bridge, there was no turning around and no second try. I was now irrevocably committed to this tenuous crossing.

My 60-lb backpack was top-heavy and a tiny slip would mean an instant deathfall into the dark abyss. A too-sudden movement or simple weight shift would result in a quick death. I knew that retrieval of my body would not be attempted. I could not afford to look down or pause as I had mild vertigo happening. I was keenly aware I had to balance perfectly and place each step correctly or die.

There was simply no margin for error. So, I moved slowly and smoothly. I recalled how I would move like slow-flowing water in the New Jersey woods to get close to whitetail deer. This was the way I moved now. My focus on staying upright was total.

In a few minutes I reached the other side, but the last move up and off the ice bridge was the crux effort. I extended my hands onto the glacier surface and leaned forward to transfer weight. The more I leaned, the more chance that my feet would slip from under me and there was nothing for my hands to grip.

Somehow, I got my torso over the glacier edge and let my chest down onto the flat ice surface. There was still nothing to pull against or push off of. I rested like that for several minutes to allow my heart rate to slow down.

As I rested, I felt a stillness between the supreme concentration now past and the effort that remained. I actually don't know how I accomplished getting off that ice bridge and onto the glacier surface. I do know that finding my inner stillness was key and that I had escaped death by the narrowest of margins.

Soon after this expedition I learned that my newlywed bride had been pregnant with our first child. What a loss that would have been for me to perish at the cusp of fatherhood!

Years later I read John Muir's account of being lost on an Alaskan glacier and having to negotiate a very similar ice bridge. He wrote more eloquently than I of the dilemma and danger. Thankfully, the world didn't lose him or me to the blue-black ice.

Personal Journaling Exercise

How often do I pause to feel my own essence and inner stillness? When and how can I make space to quiet the world for a time?

Next Step Meditation

Get into a comfortable position. Close your eyes and relax into a natural breathing pattern. Make micro-adjustments as needed (yawn, stretch, roll your shoulders).

Take a moment to allow yourself permission to take the next step on your personal evolution. Notice any tension or resistance and soften that part of your body where resistance is held.

Notice where you feel most open and relaxed. Breathe into this part of your body and allow that openness to expand. Feel the increased relaxation that comes with being more open.

Let yourself feel a "YES" for living a bigger version of you. Perhaps you can sense an increased sense of wholeness. Feel the power of your decision to align with the deeper aspects of your essence. Remain in this feeling as long as you wish.

In the coming days, cultivate gentleness with yourself. Allow yourself an easy pace for any new insights to be integrated.

Personal Journaling Exercise

Write out any message, or messages, received in this meditation.
What does my body want me to know?
Where in my body do I feel this knowing?

Your Primary Relationship Commitment

Make your primary relationship commitment be to your own clarity and integrity. Every choice you'll have today (and every day) is an opportunity to move closer or further from personal integrity. Success in this arena will come, not from what you know, it will come from what you do.

All of us have come up short in a moment of truth. The good news is that more moments are on the way. The answers are in your center, not your head. You can dig deep and be ready. You can choose presence and not run or shrink next time.

An acutely challenging situation often calls forth a person's best qualities. When the going gets tough, the true fighter keeps going.

However, the more telling test and where sustainable growth occurs, is practicing everyday toughness. A normal day is when the average person is most at risk for negotiating away the disciplines that matter. Special days, like holidays are also easier to justify letting agreements to yourself fade.

Skipping meditation or a workout are classic examples of things that are all too easy to let slide. Once you tell yourself that it is alright to pass on the difficult activity just because it is easier to wait for another time, then it will be easier to skip that discipline more and more often going forward. This is how we slowly abandon the greater version of our self that could have been. This is how we return to mediocrity.

Don't wish it was easier, wish you were better. ～ Jim Rohn

Become the person who keeps their commitments to themself. Do what you must to remove self-negotiation from the equation. Don't wake up and decide which disciplines or self-care rituals to do that day. A values-based decision is more powerful than a commitment, so pre-decide what you will make happen.

A Soul Statement can be a stock response to a recurring fearful thought or self-negotiation. By the way, I no longer use the snooze function on my alarm. This is because hitting the snooze button sends a message that I will negotiate on this time commitment.

It isn't the mountains to climb that wear you out, it's the pebble in your shoe. ～ Muhammad Ali

Our everyday opponents are believing our thoughts and self-negotiation. Counter these opponents by routinely returning to the core of who you are with a Soul Statement and notice how your day-to-day interactions change.

Let a Soul Statement impel you to take the next right action. Motivation is a bigger lift in the absence of action. So, do the actions that you promised yourself that you'd engage in and let motivation catch up. Consider that time spent in mediation or a physical workout is an investment in feeling better and in a stronger, more functional tomorrow.

Soul Statement Examples
Answers are in my center.
There is a right action I can take to support me.

Even if you do an abbreviated version of an activity, such as journaling a paragraph instead of a page or doing 5 push-ups instead of 25, your brain will maintain a congruent self-image.

The inner message will be something like, *"People like me do <this thing> even when we don't feel like it."* Be the person who keeps showing up for themself. If you cannot complete he whole task, do part of it. Just don't "do nothing".

Personal Journaling Exercise
Do I keep micro-commitments to myself when it is "just another day"?
Do I stay on track when it doesn't seem to matter or when no one is looking?
Am I being honest about my own motivation or lack thereof?

Journaling helps sustain intimacy with self. Journaling can tap into a source of *spirit water* that bubbles up from the well of mystery that you are. What might be uncovered if you journaled as a consistent, daily practice? In addition to the prompts sprinkled throughout this book, you may choose a power question and journal what comes up as a way of answering it. Remember, good questions are magnets for solutions.

Presence

Presence is a meta-skill. A meta-skill is a practiced ability that makes the rest of your life consistently better or easier. Reading is a meta-skill. Discipline is a meta-skill. Being more present for oneself allows for showing up in the moment with enhanced attention and intention.

For many years, I only showed up INSIDE my head. I would have been voted *least likely to succeed socially* in my high school yearbook, if such a category existed. I even managed to escape high school without ever initiating a conversation with a girl.

I used shyness as an excuse not to engage with others. In early adulthood, I often wondered why life didn't respond with awesomeness. My first girlfriends were women who initiated intimate contact out of exasperation that I wasn't going to make any decisive move in their direction anytime soon.

The world responds to presence and to a lack thereof very acutely. To the degree that you show up for life, life shows up for you. When you give energy, the world responds with energy. If you're hesitant to show up in the world, you're impotent in a sense.

Why not be energy-rich when you engage with life? The good news is that enhanced presence can be developed. Presence is developed, in part, by consistently connecting to, and demonstrating, your clarity and integrity.

When your partner is distressed, you can help them by remaining grounded and in your ease. This way you are being an *emotional anchor* so that they can work through being bothered and find their own ease. Show clarity, calmness and certainty to the best of your ability. In any case, your options are fear or mastery (of yourself).

Personal Journaling Exercise

Where do I give attention to things that don't serve my values or personal vision?
Is there a Soul Statement that would help anchor me to my certainty right now?

Presence in Action

I felt elevated and moved by grace as the large horse pivoted and turned under my saddle. My hands held the soft leather reins loosely, yet with confidence, as the narrow and rough trail we'd been following snaked down a thickly forested slope. She and I had learned to trust one another over time and I was keenly aware that she was paying close attention to my guidance as we navigated various trail obstacles.

I communicated primarily with my weight and my leg pressure. I gave her verbal confirmation when she moved just as I asked. The horse and I navigated through the tangle of brush and logs together, each step a conscious and important act. There was precious little room for error as the steep incline was full of obstructions. The concentration, trust and partnership was total as we worked our way through the forest.

There had been a recent storm resulting in many downed tree limbs and the ground was wet and soft. We were making deliberate progress and then encountered a large tree that had fallen across the trail. I dismounted and led the horse by a lead rope off to the side to get past the tangle. I was in a precarious position by being downslope of the horse.

In addition to route-finding, I focused on remaining calm and offering smooth movement and soothing talk. Mutual trust meant the difference between finding the trail again and a panicked 1,000-pound animal lunging right over me.

At one point the horse put a rear hoof into a slot between two tree branches and was momentarily trapped in place. I saw her immediately tense up. This was the moment of truth. The horse held her position and looked to me for direction. I kept talking in a gentle, slow tone of voice. I held an inner stillness as I knew the horse was taking the cue for what to do next from my movements and my energy.

Thankfully, the horse felt and responded to my calm instruction and allowed me to direct her next steps beyond the trouble. At the bottom of the slope, I got back into the saddle and finished the ride home.

Any intimate companion deserves your presence and ease in the form of a light heart, open ears and an uncluttered mind. Openhearted listening without a personal agenda is true listening. Learn to hold space for your own feelings without going for a roller coaster ride with them.

When a friend comes to you with an issue and you don't know what to say, drop in and offer more of you. Say a Soul Statement inwardly. Tune in to your center. Dial up your presence and just listen.

Being connected on the inside and congruent on the outside is what I call broadcasting on your own frequency. Telling the truth about yourself on the inside with a Soul Statement is a way to stay tuned to this personal frequency. All Corey, all the time, is the frequency that works best for Corey. Stay tuned to yourself.

Soul Statement Examples

A strong, still place is at my core.
My soul has certainty.
Strength is within me.

Body Cues

Body cues can confirm when you're more grounded in your personal power. For me, one of the more obvious clues that I've stepped into deeper self-connectedness is that my voice pitch and tone will deepen. When the tempo of my speech becomes more deliberate, my whole body feels more substantial and solid. I can also deepen my voice first in order to drop in below the concern of the moment into a more self-connected state.

There is more wisdom in your body than in
your deepest philosophy.~ Friedrich Nietzsche

Let your own body cues be a reminder to make adjustments (voice, posture, etc.) and use a Soul Statement as needed to anchor into your body, your presence and the present moment. When you're in a really good state, use a Soul Statement to keep the momentum going in a good direction.

Personal Journaling Exercise

What are my body cues?

Stopping Resistance

It was a hot day in the Pine Barrens and a fast-moving, spring-fed creek formed a deep pool near where our group rested. The crystal-clear water was tantalizing, but the chilly water temperature was quite daunting. Not one person was getting in the water, but I made a decision to get to know cold even though I was afraid of it.

I stepped to the edge of the creek, took a deep breath, slid into the water and let my body sink to the sandy bottom. It was quiet and still and so very cold. I gave in and let the cold absorb into me. The cold and I became as one. I couldn't be hurt by what was now me. I knew cold from a different perspective and saw that it only caused pain when I resisted it.

Years later, in Utah, I sat on a rock at the edge of Blue Lake (10,700 feet above sea level). This lake was formed of snowmelt seeping from under an adjacent rock slope. The high cliff band of the mountain summit loomed far above. As I sat there, I became willing to turn my life over in service to a Higher Power by a ceremony of self-baptism.

I remembered that icy, clear creek years ago in the Pine Barrens and chose to enter the near-freezing water of Blue Lake. The water was terribly, unfeelingly cold and my body braced against it, but I knew to stop resisting and relax. As I surrendered to the experience, cold enveloped me and I felt imbued with its impassive strength. I can feel that strength even now.

When you connect to who and what you are, you more easily live in congruence with your nature. Re-orienting takes ongoing discipline and heart, but part of your job is to stop resisting. Just as an unplugged lamp is simply a coat rack, the unplugged person's light is dim. When you catch a glimpse of your personal North Star, keep re-orienting to it. Trust the wisdom that created you.

My close friends and I celebrate and welcome emotions. We find emotional safety in speaking true and communicating true. Paying attention to what you have energy for, and acting on or speaking to that, leads to more rewarding choices and invitations. Whatever you are doing, feeling the associated emotion will take you into a richer experience.

Chapter Summary

Make your primary commitment to your own clarity and truth. Focus on what's most right about you and live as your unique and true expression. Inner stillness is an offering that you can gift to yourself.

Honesty with self is power. The answers are in your center, not your head. Your body, and the moment, is where truth lives. Find the moment and you win.

Embrace challenges, create healthy structure and look to be the right person. A bigger you lives! The world will respond to what you are on the inside.

Practice everyday toughness. All you will ever need is already within you. It's time to stop paying attention to whatever is not you.

In the next chapter we'll explore how to go deep and remain connected to your center of gravity (while staying light). There will be more tools for turning on your power, including, enhancing inner stillness, connecting to your body and honoring emotions.

If you are moved to, tag me in a social media post saying, "*Yes*" to finding answers in your center and standing in your truth, with the hashtags #innerstrength #therealme

GOING DEEP

Within you, there is a stillness and a sanctuary to which you can retreat at any time and be yourself. ~ Hermann Hesse

It is natural to ebb and flow with attention as one gets absorbed in demands and distractions of the day. Spinning up with events or busy-ness is all too easy. There remains a deep part of you that never forgets who and what you are. Declaring a Soul Statement is a way to tap into your soul wisdom as needed to inform your present experience and next right action.

Soul Statement Example
My inner knowing is available to me.

The counter-balance to distraction is to slow down and deeply listen to one's center. Practice slowing down by simply taking a bit of time to close your eyes and watch your breath. Just breathe and allow your awareness to sink beneath surface thoughts.

Sometimes I will visualize my mind as a muddy glass of water that is becoming clear as the dirt particles settle to the bottom. I'll allow my thoughts to settle along with the contents of this imaginary glass.

I thoroughly enjoy bodysurfing in the ocean. It is often prudent to dive underneath the biggest waves. So, I'll press my body on the sandy bottom and listen to the profound silence as the wave rolls by above me.

Finding the deeper you is a lot like diving under a wave and listening to the ocean silence. During my silent devotion in the mornings, I often recall the feeling of the silence under the surface of the ocean to help me feel the quiet that exists under my surface thoughts.

Soul Statement Examples
Stillness is my natural home.
Silence is always present.

Silence is a sanctuary from story and worry. The place inside that feels like home (where everything is okay) is a wonderful place to keep returning to. Drop in and find your home for just a moment.

Home is where you are in touch with who you really are. Simply pausing to remember who you are at depth may be all you have to do to increase serenity and optimism.

Your soul has answers that silence lets you hear. The place of information beyond words is so close, but it must be consciously sought in the waking state. Could you take a few moments each day to gather a bit of your personal essence? You may come to love contacting the great silence that lives under everyday perception.

Almost everything will work again if you unplug it
for a few minutes, including you. ~ Anne Lamont

When I inwardly say the Soul Statement, "**The contentment of the mountains lives within me**", I feel the truth of it in my cells. Where were you when you felt the most content? I invite you to drop in to your own quiet place to find your serenity. The more you do this, the more accessible contentment will become.

Claiming the deep within (my term for contacting one's center) doesn't require a large time commitment, just consistent time for internal connection. Noticing that you are *off* is a signal to pause and connect inwardly. Make some of your alone time into soul time.

You may duck out of a stressful situation as needed to re-center and align with the deep that lives within you. A silent Soul Statement can help you find a still place within when it is not practical to be alone.

Soul Statement Examples

Quiet soothes me.
Silence holds answers.

A couple whom I was coaching was feeling isolated within their marriage. Their desired closeness and connection was no longer present. She often threatened a complete separation (divorce) and he shut down further when hearing that ultimatum. This triggered her more deeply into feeling lonely.

A true *misery-go-round* was occurring. Under my direction, they each found a Soul Statement to apply when doubting their value. She chose, "**I am safe and worthy of love.**" He chose, "**I can handle whatever comes.**"

These Soul Statements allowed for a measure of inner calm so they could talk without running away. I also led them through an exercise (called, "*If you really knew me*") in order to foster empathy and patience.

Once they re-connected to who they really were, further techniques or practices were of secondary importance. They went on to have needed and meaningful conversations with each other while maintaining mutual respect.

Tantra

Living tantra is choosing an openness to life that weaves itself into thought, emotion and action. Tantra is essentially an attitude and practice of paying attention to the moment. The more deeply you inhabit the moment, the more you are being tantric. We all know intuitively that the spark of the Divine is inside us. The task, or Divine Invitation, is to live this knowing at our surface.

During my first tantric temple experience, my companion and I sat in utter stillness and gazed into each other's eyes. Everything outside of our immediate space ceased to exist. It felt to me that the air in the room had been replaced by a breathable joy.

We held compassion for each other as emotions were released. We flowed easily from stillness to movement and back to stillness. We felt connected to the immense, breathing earth and to the light in our hearts. In this ritual dance, I felt somehow changed at the molecular level. It felt like all of my essence 'arrived' all at once.

The essential experience of coming home to myself that I awoke to in that tantra ceremony has remained accessible ever since. Recalling the feeling of that experience helps call up the grounded, connected-to-my-soul me.

Each of us has a day or a moment when we came the closest to feeling our soul-essence. Your essence can be called forth and claimed. This is what spiritual teachers speak of when they say, "*dig deep and touch the fire in your belly.*"

Soul Statement Examples
Peace is here.
My body is truth.

Inner Movement Meditation
Find a comfortable position for your body and close your eyes. Make micro-adjustments as needed (yawn, stretch, roll your shoulders...) Allow your breath to find a natural rhythm. Keep your attention on your breath and notice the quality of your breath.

Build awareness of where the breath goes inside your body. Become more aware of your depth. Feel for your essence, the way a bear may feel the coming change of season. Notice your inner weather.

Sense the currents of energy inside your body. Take a few breaths to really feel beneath and beyond words. Stay open to a message or emotion from any area of your body.

Remain in this open state as long as you wish.

Stop, Drop and Roll
I like the term **Stop, Drop** and **Roll** as shorthand for getting quiet and getting connected. By slowing down, we can better feel who, what and why we are. **STOP** and press pause on external input. **DROP** into your quiet center. **ROLL** with what shows up. Even the briefest moment with your soul has outsized benefit.

What if knowing yourself at depth produced a state of
immovable joy at your surface?

One of my favorite things to do is lie on my belly and gaze into a natural spring. I never tire of watching water emerge from the sandy bottom. The water rises without cease as a constant, copious and free gift of life.

In a highly-connected state, one's soul is bubbling with knowing, inspiration and optimism like a flowing spring of water. You deserve to inhabit this state that is your natural home.

Personal Journaling Exercise

What is a good Soul Statement to help me DROP?

In his *Vision Quest* song, John Dupuy sings, "*...like water from a spring I've always known.*" That's what it feels like when the deep me bubbles up to the surface – like finding a part of me I've always known. When one doesn't identify and claim their birthright as a free soul, they don't live the bigger life that could have been.

Soul Statement Examples

I can let the knowing of my spirit bubble up from inside me.
There is a wellspring of creativity inside me.
I have a place and a destiny in this world.

Getting to the Bullseye

As a scrawny, shy, 13-year-old boy scout I was part of a troop represent-ing the USA at the 1977 Canadian National Jamboree on Prince Edward Island. One activity was an archery station where each boy could shoot one arrow. In the hour that I waited in line not one person hit the center of the target.

Then an older boy just ahead of me nailed a perfect dead-center bullseye shot. The counselors and crowd cheered in celebration and respect. That boy then turned and handed me the bow with a sneer saying, "I bet ya can't

Robinhood that one." (My uniform identified me as the lone American at that activity station.)

I said nothing, stepped up to the line and let a bubble of quiet surround me. The target was my complete and only focus. In drew the bowstring back and breathed out as I released the arrow. My arrow hit the dead-center bullseye, splitting the previous one down the middle.

Splitting an arrowshaft lengthwise on a dead-center shot is known as a "Robinhood". The onlookers were stunned at this unexpected event and no one spoke. I just set the bow down and walked away. Sadly, my friends back at camp did not believe this story. They only saw me as a goofy kid and had no idea what I was capable of under the surface.

Sometimes life says, "*Step up!*" and, when we answer, the result can transcend everyday ability. We are all capable of getting to the bullseye, to what is most important, when we slow down and tune in. The body and mind acting in resonance is capable of accomplishing remarkable tasks.

At the archery station, my everyday mind had to suspend thinking and let a deeper state be dominant. I knew the truth of what I could do in my nervous system, in my bones and my muscles. I wanted to show the sneering Canadians that American boys are as good as they. That day I did something amazing when my head got out of the way.

Soul Statement Example

There is peace and stillness at my center.

When you slow down enough to be connected to your inner calm, the outer life naturally slows down a notch or two. The world is still spinning, but there is peace and comfort in knowing where your center is. Your heart always knows what really matters. When your heart's frequency matches your actions, words and thoughts, an inner peace and contentment comes with it.

Personal Journaling Exercise
Things in my life that are unattractive to me are...
What version of me best serves the world?

Speaking truth to yourself activates personal power and happiness is dialed up by doing so. The feelings that result for many people is of being ultra-centered, clear, grounded and sure. When you know who and what you are at depth, you can more easily drop the overlay of habits and conditioning. **Every moment is an invitation to be more present.** Every moment is a chance to be more integrated with your body, heart and right action.

Soul Statement Example
My values are important and valid.

A Soul Statement and the feeling that goes with it is a way for your heart to inform your brain that the center of gravity is lower in your body than your head. A Soul Statement is a postcard from a better emotional address, saying, *"Here is where you belong."*

As you apply a practice here and a tool there at some point you're no longer practicing. It is your new normal. Consistently applied tools become habits. Your habits become who you are. In this way, you may claim *the deep* within. You'll be in alignment with what Martha Beck terms the *"meta-self."*

Use a Soul Statement when you catch yourself wandering off track. You may catch yourself wandering again moments later and that is okay. Just keep returning to inner alignment. Like a boat captain who must constantly adjust the rudder to stay on a desired heading in the sea, we all have micro-adjustments to make.

Soul Statement Example
My inner alignment is always available.

Don't let a thought that would bring you down stand unchallenged. Make your next thought a better one. The Soul Statement, **"My body heals quickly and well"**, can override the unhelpful thought, *"This condition could bring me down."* Repeating a Soul Statement lets your most helpful messages sink in.

Personal Journaling Exercise
Am I using my current thought to grow or am I feeling poorly?
Does this thought empower or disempower me?
If I changed my thinking about this, what would be possible?

Just Being Meditation
Close your eyes and breathe naturally without effort. Place a hand on your heart and just feel. Breathe into your heart. Realize that your heart beats with or without your attention or effort. Consider that it has kept you alive since before birth. Just keep breathing without effort.

You may ask your heart to share its wisdom at this time. Remain open to a message from your heart. Allow for a gentle awakening of your essential essence with each breath.

Now, allow yourself to be flooded with the feeling of having and being what you want. Let positivity wash through your body and immediate field. Inhabit a bigger version of you as you imagine occupying your right place in the world.

When you deeply feel your worth, you may have tears well up. It may seem like this world is finally a home. You may experience an unfamiliar current of energy in your body.

Allow the power of this state to open your heart. Let yourself feel relaxed and unstoppable. The more you inhabit this feeling, the better you'll be able to call forth this state as needed.

You may come back to this mediation again and again and observe how your openness expands with what you believe is possible for your experience of life.

Why should anyone else treat you better than you treat yourself? The good news is that you get to set the tone for how the world treats you. Remember that your worth does not have to be related to anything that you do. You are a worthy *being*, not just a human *doing*.

Soul Statement Examples
My emotions are precious and connected to my power.
When my head and heart are connected, I am brave
and unstoppable.

Current feelings create an emotional escrow account. In other words, your future experience will most certainly match the dominant feelings that you hold. Keep in mind that the feeling that your thoughts generate is more important than the thought itself.

Emotion is what informs your subconscious and affects change. Emotion is what will translate to your bones and nervous system and to an invisible escrow account of attraction. An emotion that is felt weakly, will have a correspondingly lesser effect.

Be nurturing to your neurology. Emotions are precious. They connect you to your power. Holding on to energy that doesn't serve you is costly. To get from head to heart, remind yourself to *just feel*. When connected to your heart, you'll be a bit braver than you were before. When you increase kindness on the inside, you'll naturally treat other people better.

Forgive and Love

Most of my life I played small. I was afraid of my own bigger expression and exuberance. There were years when I didn't allow myself bigger dreams because I was afraid and confused of how I could get there. I did not compete with what I was capable of. I did not even ask myself what I wanted most. I let my imagination atrophy. I diminished my desires. I was the polite guy with few needs.

Waking up to the truth of your worth might involve forgiving yourself for previously operating from false notions. When we offer ourselves compassion, we heal on the inside. If self-forgiveness feels like a big lift (as it did for me at first) you might start with self-acceptance as I did.

Quite simply, loving yourself begins with loving yourself even when you don't want to. (Thank you, Stan Dale.) Just as an electrical dimmer switch adjusts the light by increasing or decreasing resistance to the power supply, you may increase your available personal power by decreasing inner resistance.

Soul Statement Examples

Playing small does not serve me.
My exuberance is a gift.
I can live unafraid.

It takes courage to own your motivations. It also takes courage to own your impact when your actions have been injurious. However, this level of honesty is critical to a life of personal power. Every moment is a date with your power. You can turn away or take the opportunity to tell the truth on the inside. Speaking truth with kindness and clarity can enhance inner and outer connection. Messy truth can sometimes be an aphrodisiac!

The Truth Shall Set You Free.

Actively practice softening your mind and heart. With softness, comes easier acceptance of what is occurring in real time. The goal is not to 'fix' any given interaction or to change another person. It's enough to simply live in an alive, embodied present. This is part of how you keep the #TheRealYou once you find him or her.

Personal Journaling Exercise
Do I typically appreciate insight, but continue as before?
Could I become willing to allow discomfort in order to
feel what is underneath it?

You can watch your energy circle the proverbial drain when focusing on what's wrong. You can also apply tools to lift yourself out of an old story and bring attention to what is right. You can choose to connect to your soul and body wisdom. A potent state is always available.

Integrated clarity calls up the best version of you. The big question in any given moment is whether you will step up and claim yourself. Happiness is a decision. Make a commitment to your own sovereignty and clarity. Being resourced from within serves you and everyone that you interact with.

Soul Statement Examples
The Real Me is enough.
When I trust my inner voice, I have better outcomes.

One day, while I was building an addition on our home and was working on the roof, my contractor shouted up to me that he was leaving for lunch. After a few moments the question popped into my head, "Where is Cree?". (Cree was my 2 ½ year old son.) This question came with a gut feeling of extreme urgency.

Without hesitation, I hurried off the roof via a ladder and sprinted to the driveway. I had no plan other than that I had to find my son right away. I rounded the corner of the home as the man was starting his van. He saw me and I waved my arms at him to wait.

I found Cree sitting on his little tricycle just a foot away from the rear of the van. He had the tricycle parked in the exact center of the bumper, right behind the trailer hitch. The driver had no view of him in any mirror.

I scooped up my son and carried him to the side and then let the driver back up onto the street. Whew! What a close call! A powerful lesson to trust my inner voice, for sure. A part of me didn't want the inconvenience of pausing my work and finding my child. Nevertheless, the feeling was too strong to negotiate away. Luckily, my soul is connected to my son and his well-being on a deep level.

The Sanskrit word, *Shanti*, specifically translates as, *The Peace That Comes from Knowing Who You Are.* A great gift to give yourself and others is a peaceful mind. I am a fan of stillness as its own practice. Stillness can be a form of soul-nourishment. Stillness can be its own prayer.

I will often stand or sit in front of my home altar or a beautiful place in nature and simply offer my stillness. A Soul Statement may spontaneously arise during stillness. How might your beloved respond if you met them with deep stillness?

Personal Journaling Exercise

How often do I pause to feel my inner silence?
When and how can I make space to quiet the world
for a time each day?

Short-Term Discomfort

My first Junior High dance was an awkward experience of taking a really long time to ask a girl to slowdance and then not knowing how to move. I also wondered if and how we might kiss, since I had no prior romantic experience. Even though a lot of it was uncomfortable, I was proud of myself for initiating a dance.

The next day, at breakfast, my parents asked me how it went. I told them and they laughed. Their laughter felt really awful at the time, but I realize now that they were happy for me and the joviality stemmed from their own awkwardness around the subject of my dating.

Sadly, I never went to another dance or asked a girl out during my remaining school years. I was simply unwilling to risk the feeling of being laughed at by my parents again.

Living with short-term discomfort is another meta-skill. I lived the bulk of my early life with a primary goal of avoiding embarrassment. I really dislike the feeling of, '*I'm bare-assed*'. It is normal to want to shrink or hide when fear grabs hold of your psyche. Embarrassment is another manifestation of fear.

Strong feelings can inform a you of a deeper story or program that is running in the background. This programming uses up your energy in the same way that a phone app drains battery life even when you're not interfacing with it. **What we tell ourselves on the inside matters**. We must tolerate some discomfort by telling the truth in order to know our self with more clarity.

Give yourself permission to experience discomfort in order to know your truth. It is okay to sit with confusion or tension and not do anything about it. Don't just identify a feeling and move on.

Let your emotions inform you. Feel each emotion as fully as you are able.

It is often helpful to decide a time-frame to be with hard-to-feel feelings. For example, *"I will allow X feeling to wash over me for the next 30 minutes and then I will put it aside for the time being."* Journaling this emotional process can be a rich source of insight.

Soul Statement Examples
I am nourished by stillness.
I have clarity and sureness within.

Chapter Summary
Make it a habit to access inner stillness and touch the sanctuary within. Silence is healing. Silence holds answers. **Stop**, **Drop** and **Roll** as needed.

Align with your truth. It takes bravery to go deep. It takes bravery to claim your space and your needs. When you do so, you'll find that people who appreciate depth, bravery and kindness will gravitate to you. People who don't will fade from your sphere. If everyone spoke only what is true, brave and kind we would change the world.

All external experience is a mirror. You can feel or fold. You can spin or find solution. You can go to shame or freedom. You can learn to live with a bit of discomfort. Every difficulty is a lesson in becoming who and what you are capable of.

Carpe Diem! ~ Seize the Day!
Carpe Abyssi! ~ Seize the Deep!

Happiness is less an objective reality than a subjective decision. Keep your emotional pantry stocked. Stand in your clarity. Rest in your knowing. Offer silence at your personal altar or in nature. Every moment is an invitation to be more present.

In the next chapter we'll explore how to interrupt your story and be kind with fear. We'll address the importance of acting as your own best friend. You'll gain insight and tools to embrace the unapologetic you that says, "*No*" to everything that is not your truth or joy.

If you are moved to, tag me in a social media post claiming your place in this world, with the hashtags #innerwisdom #iamhome

5

❦

CONVERSATION WITH SELF

If being hard on yourself was going to work,
it would have worked by now. ~ Mel Robbins

Conversations will determine the direction of your star. The most important conversations you will ever have will be with the voice in your own head. What you say on the inside has a profound impact on what you believe you're capable of and what you expect to experience. Soul Statements will up-level your inner conversations.

Soul Statement Example
What's right is always available to me.

The sheer volume of self-talk (thousands of thoughts a day) reinforces beliefs that each of us hold. The bulk of those thoughts are repeats from the day before and the day before that. Replaying

51

outdated stories keeps a person running in circles or even circling the proverbial drain. Since inner dialog is happening as an almost constant narration, why not bring attention and intention to bear and give your brain a better conversation? Using a Soul Statement is a way to re-direct one's thinking from a surface concern to something positive and unchanging.

Soul Statement Example

My soul knows what to do.

We all regulate our experience by behaving in congruence with what we believe deep down. Each of us has a mental belief structure that wants to remain sane. The brain accomplishes this by creating congruency with inner expectation and outer experience.

For example, kindness is part of who I think I am. So, to act in an unkind way I'd have to alter what I believe about myself or tell myself a story about making an exception.

Self-talk accumulates in the brain and your subconscious mind will believe what your conscious mind tells it. In *The Biology of Belief*, Bruce H. Lipton, Ph.D. writes: *Our cells are eavesdropping on our thoughts.* The subconscious part of your brain wants to make sure that your thinking is in line with what you already believe so that it can set your thermostat of life to just the right emotional temperature. You will experience what you believe to be true.

The better my story gets, the better my life gets.

Dr. Joe Dispenza says, "*Feelings are the language of the body*". What we focus on determines our emotional state. Our emotional state will determine our activity and choices. We think with words and convert them to images, which are then converted to emotions. Emotions become our reality.

Our minds are designed and primed to look for what is wrong. The good news is that what's right in any given moment is always there to be recognized and claimed. We don't get what we want in life, we get that which we feel we deserve. This is a key reason why making regular Soul Statements is important.

What internal state do you want to operate from more of the time? What if you lived with an open, generous heart contained in a resourced, safe, adult perspective? What if you reminded yourself each day of what is really so? What if you could shift out of distress more easily?

Since we're not on a treeless tundra being stalked by short-faced bears and sabertooth cats, perhaps the alert status can drop from orange to green? Distance allows perspective. Perspective allows insight. Insight allows for a shift in emotional state. Fresh insight and different emotions should, ideally, lead to improved actions. New and better actions should serve greater insight and feelings as a positive feedback loop.

Soul Statement Examples
My fears do not define me.
I have all the resources I need within me.
I can choose better thoughts.

Your subconscious is observing all your thoughts and feelings. It is filtering for experiences within the range that you've determined as acceptable. In order to upgrade to a better experience of life one must inform the subconscious and update its operating program.

There is a Goldilocks Zone of what we believe we are worthy of. (A Goldilocks Zone describes where it is not too hot nor too cold and not to soft nor too hard.) Most people can't let themselves be too successful or ecstatic. Conversely, most of us don't let our experience become too utterly wretched, either.

Any newly expanded awareness must be incorporated and accommodated at the level of belief in order for us to keep it. Each of us can do a better job of curating our internal playlist. One way to do this is by consistently inserting desired messages to counteract previously unchallenged thoughts. These are the thoughts that arise from outdated beliefs.

Make your second thought a better one than your first (default) thought. Persist in the practice of focusing on your deepest, most relevant value and, over time, your default thought will be more aligned with who you really are.

Soul Statement Examples
I can curate and direct my thinking in a good direction.
I always have a better thought to opt into.

When we feel good and connected to right purpose we can step up and handle just about anything. When we feel down, stressed or adrift, we cannot handle much at all. In a connected state we get solutions. In a miserable state we get drama. The upshot is that you don't need to fight old thought patterns, just replace them with thoughts that are more optimistic and loving.

> *Incremental improvement is what allows us to*
> *do great things over time. ~ Tim Ferriss*

Judgements, Beliefs and Stories

It is helpful to think about when you formed a given judgment and why. When did you last update a belief that you took on in childhood? The young sage, Freedom Franklin, says, *"Break up with each unhelpful story like it is a bad relationship that no longer serves you."*

Think about what you would hope for your own children or grandchildren. Do you wish them a smaller or larger expression of their essential nature? In what ways could you model a higher expression for the special people in your life?

Personal Journaling Exercise

What I believe I'm capable of is...

Stories move us away from the bull's-eye of what we're feeling and needing. Inner dialog can be your worst enemy and lead you over the cliff of despair. Inner dialog can also be your ally and a lifeline to a better life. Just keep reminding your internal voice (with love) that this is not story time and re-align with a Soul Statement.

The mind often acts like a music player with one or two songs stuck on a loop. These songs (stories) are maintaining the status quo, until you notice and supplant them. Instead of replaying an old story, simply anchor to who you are. For example, a great goal is to shrink, and eventually eliminate, internal sarcasm and belittling.

When you find yourself holding an old assumption or judgment, choose to insert an updated version in its place. You might need to remind your Inner Judge that, *"Court is not in session"*.

Personal Journaling Exercise (repeat as needed)

Does the story I'm running lead me higher or lower?
I'm story-telling right now. What's really true is...
I hear that and what's really true is...

Fold or Focus

It was a perfect day for rock climbing – bright sun, clean sandstone and a technically competent friend. I began the lead ascent off the ground in order to bring the rope to a permanent anchor high on the steep cliff. The plan was for my companion to then work their way up to join me whilst safely protected by my secure rope attachment from above.

I connected the rope to the rock anchors about every 15 feet as I moved higher. Climbing past a last rope connection on a vertical rock face is exciting at first, but as one continues upward, the negative repercussions of a fall drastically increase.

At 55 feet above the ground, I got to a rest spot of sorts and palpable fear took over my body. If I slipped here, the best-case outcome was a 30-foot fall. My anxiety spiked and my legs began to shake. I was dependent on a ½" wide toehold for my feet, a fingertip grip for one hand and nothing but a pressure smear on the smooth cliff face for the other hand. My options were focus in right now or take a big fall in a second or three.

The voice in my head spoke up and said, "You're not a rock climber. What are you doing up here? This is way too scary! You are NOT a rock climber." I made a conscious decision to press pause on this fearful self-talk and metaphorically place the fear in my back pocket. When I did so, the shaking in my legs stopped. Now, I could better focus on the micro-texture of this cliff that I could press onto.

Fear can stand for 'Forget Everything and Run' or 'Face Everything and Respond'. I took a couple seconds to decide the move sequence and then executed upward. The next secure anchor connection for my rope had been only about four feet above my head, but if I had let fear prevail, I would not have made it safely there.

When your doubt arises and the familiar voice inside your head says, *"I'm not <this thing>!"* Or, *"People like me can't do this!"* Say to your thinking brain, *"Not today. We can talk about this later. Right now, I'm going to focus in."* Then do what you must to meet that particular challenge.

Soul Statement Example

My deep sureness is more powerful than my surface thoughts.

Be Kind with Fear

You don't want the fearful parts of you to make your decisions. The ego is not a source of solutions. This being said, be kind with your concerns when they come up. It may be useful to forgive yourself for giving in to a particular fear in the past. Treat feelings as signals, not enemies. **It is appropriate to give fear a voice, but not to give it veto power**.

My clients consistently find it helpful to acknowledge the pure desire hidden inside a wounded feeling. I will then guide them into offering compassion for this concerned aspect. When a hurt feeling is acknowledged and honored, it can be put in its right context and perspective.

Why not wring out the useful takeaway in a given episode that may have caused you to stumble in the past? Commit to re-patterning when you reach a new choice point. By listening to the source inside, you may stop outsourcing your own well-being. The alternative is to repeat experiences over and over. Put your brain and your heart on the same team. In this way, you can more readily generate right action.

Soul Statement Examples

My fear gets a voice, but not a vote.
I am stronger and wiser than my fearful thoughts.

Beautiful Dreams (that didn't happen)

As a young man with a newborn son, I was filled with a desire to give him an immersion experience of nature. This type of deep dive into wild and remote country had so often had fed my own soul. I wanted to spend an entire summer together as a small family in the wilderness.

I imagined us gathering food and living with nature's rhythm as the ancient inhabitants had. My wife was 100 percent on board. We decided to put it off until our boy was 4 years old (just before he would enter the school system).

Year three welcomed a new baby. My three-year-old now had a little brother. We could still have gone into the wilderness that next summer. We knew where to make our base camp. We had the open schedule. We had funds to cover bills. We had spiritual alignment. We did NOT do advance planning. We did NOT put it on the calendar. There was no big argument or disagreement. The dream just passed us by. It didn't happen.

Fast-forward twenty-five years. I'm planning an epic 140-mile solo transect of the Cabeza Prieta from Yuma to Ajo, Arizona. Basically, a whole lot of cactus, rugged mountains, sand and sky. A place to hear the great silence. A place to hear my soul speak.

Secret waterholes lie tucked away in easy-to-miss canyons. It is the last refuge for Sonoran pronghorn antelope and desert big-horn sheep. Ancient writing and millennia-old footpaths are still to be found there. Tarantulas, rattlesnakes and scorpions call this area home. Unexploded ordinance from decades of military bomb training lies scattered across the flats.

This great sweep of country was a land of healing for George Hayduke and is the final resting place of Edward Abbey. Space and more space is sheltered from human intrusion out there. The Cabeza Prieta has been described as the middle of nowhere and the center of everywhere. I've thought that I would do this trip before I die. Perhaps I would even die in the Cabeza Prieta.

I pored over maps. I researched whether to apply for a hiking permit or go commando. I thought through drop-off and pickup arrangements. I calculated the weight and bulk of the supplies for twenty-plus days of desert exploring. I conceptualized and designed a tow-behind cart to transport supplies as I'm unable to carry a backpack, due to injuries. A friend agreed to pick me up in Ajo, Arizona.

I thought about the fact that the most reliable water is monitored by illicit travel lookouts and border patrol agents – both heavily armed. Would I run the plains at night and sleep in mountains by day like an Apache scout? Should I bring along a milking goat or a pack llama? There is no serum for a sidewinder bite (not that anyone would know if I was bitten). I even outlined the class I'd later teach at an aboriginal living skills conference on extended desert trekking.

None of this mattered, as I did not go. I ran into the issue of building the cart. I did not bring resourcefulness to bear. I would need resourcefulness out there in the Back of Beyond. I didn't make a clear signal to begin. I did not decide an expedition start date and work a timeline backwards for when to get things ready. Life kept going and I did not set the time aside. I let this agenda be subsumed by life. I didn't step up, grab my desire by the throat and say, "*You're mine.*"

The bottom line is that I did not do the work to quiet my trepidation of this solo expedition. I could've named what I was afraid of (smugglers, rattlesnakes, scorpions, getting injured) and owned the fear. Instead, the cart problem was a good enough excuse.

As a result of not being honest with myself, the endeavor became a creative miscarriage. The fantasy of making something happen someday is a non-starter until one faces the reason why it hadn't happened already. In the end I performed a ritual release of this trip in order to free up creative juice for a more doable adventure.

Soul Statement Example
My dreams are important.

Be Your Own Best Friend

I often help clients recognize where they're not treating themselves as their own best friend. A good starting point is self-compassion. Can you accept that you've done your best? Can you feel compassion for the part of you that sometimes doesn't know what to do or is afraid? Applying compassion to fear and doubt is a type of psychic salve.

Love yourself and you will be invincible. ~ Jen Sincero

Each of us sets the tone for how we are treated in the world. Would you stick around a friend who talks to you the way you talk to yourself? What might change if you consistently speak to yourself as your own best friend?

What might happen if you increase compassion in your self-talk? How might your self-image improve if you add an extra dose of resourcefulness to what you already tell your own brain? Why not make your brain an ally in the effort to claim your power?

Soul Statement Examples

I have compassion for myself and what I've been through.
I am always lovable (even when I forget that this is true).

The Power of Self-Care

Self-care reunites you with what you value and is foundational to an intentional life. Knowing your most important values helps to determine priorities. Life works well to the extent that self-care is a priority. Tasks, and more tasks, are always there to consume your time if you let them.

Making your self-care non-negotiable will allow you to super-charge your experience of life. A good aspiration is to live at the right pace of life. How can you offer the world value if you never tap into the value inside you? What to do next is a simpler decision when you are in touch with what's most important. Values first. Priorities second

Intimacy with self means being connected to what's alive inside and taking appropriate steps to honor one's own needs. One friend of mine is a great role model as he lives his days in slow-motion ease and gets more accomplished in a day than most people do in three days. People and opportunities gravitate to him since others want to be around his energy and integrity.

Extreme self-care makes this man attractive. He awakens early to devote time to his spiritual connection. He may journal, walk in nature or meditate for inspiration. He forms a mental map of what he expects to unfold that day and commits to an intention of how he wants to move through each part.

Soul Statement Example
Self-care feeds my spirit.

Checkup from the Ground Up
Make mini-breaks in the day to briefly pause and plug in. Think of these breaks as a *checkup from the ground up*. Simply take a moment to speak to the rushed or worried part of you and offer a Soul Statement to replace unhelpful thoughts.

This brief soul ritual is a way to honor your heart and put what's true at the forefront of your attention. This doesn't always mean expressing your inner world directly to others. It means that you remain aligned with who you know yourself to be. It is a way to revolve around your own axis.

Soul Statement Examples
The secure part of me is more powerful than the worried part.
My self-care makes me more attractive.

I've identified my personal enemies. They are: sugar, stress, sloth and spinning (in circles). My personal saviors are: sleep, slowing down, stillness, stretching, strength-training, Source, sex, smoothies, strategy, support and significance. In addition, sacred, slow time keeps me on my inner axis.

Personal Journaling Exercise
My personal enemies are...
What depletes me or feels like an unwanted obligation?
My personal saviors are...
What renews me?

Self-Connection and Renewal
Moving at the pace of the natural world is conducive to self-reflection. Time in nature is a form of nourishment for me. I cherish my personal renewal days in nature. I may sit on a grassy hill watching a hawk unhurriedly ride unseen air currents with the shining ocean in the distance. I may enjoy a hot spring soak after a hike.

Often, I'll just sit in the sun by a running watercourse and observe the creatures that live there. Nature may be found on an apartment balcony or city park or by simply gazing at the sky. Any wild creature, even a pigeon flying by, is tapped into greater mystery and to the earth's rhythm.

Once again, the writing of Barry Lopez is illuminating. *"Intimacy with the physical Earth apparently awakens in us, at some wordless level, a primal knowledge of the nature of our emotional as well as our biological attachments to physical landscapes. ...my impression is that we experience this primal connection regularly as a diffuse, ineffable pleasure, experience it as the easing of a particular kind of longing."*

Consider spending time in your center as a form of self-respect and necessary to your well-being. Renewal days streamline connection to the inner still place so that it becomes more easily accessible going forward. As important as renewal time is, it generally won't happen unless it is blocked out on your calendar.

Personal Journaling Exercise
I am renewed by the following activities...
I will make time for my renewal activities as follows...

It may be helpful to analyze your typical week in terms of self-care. What tends to take you off your plan? How do you handle other people's emergencies? Observe how your time is sucked away (or given away) and consider where you might employ greater self-care.

Pre-decide how you will stand up for your time. Let each self-care commitment be an immovable boulder that the water of life has to flow around. An example of how one might stand up for a self-care commitment is, *"Not to be rude, but I need to take some time right now."* Or, *"I must attend to other business right now. I trust that you'll find a resolution."*

The goal of the news is to make every problem, your problem.
~ Jim Kwik

Calling forth a personal Soul Statement is a quick path to self-connection. To remain even more available for yourself, rest in deep connection at least once every day. This practice enhances your ability to dial up presence. Who is more attractive – the scattered person or the energetically contained person?

Daily self-connection practices that I enjoy are: zazen breathing, gratitude, Soul Statements, listening to bi-aural meditation soundtracks, moving my body, strength training, stretching and journaling.

I take one day each week as a renewal day where I stay offline. My phone is on airplane mode in the evening and until I'm done with my morning routine. Sundays are set aside for special connecting with my beloved. Devices are kept off on Sunday as a *Digital Sabbath*.

> *The job of the student is to show up on time.*
> *The job of the master is to arrive centered. ~ Charles Muir*

Self-care doesn't happen unless and until one makes time for it. Solo practice often needs to be supported by better time management and boundary-setting. My greater personal self-care list includes, but is not limited to: altar time, exercise, stretching, alone time on a project, love connection with my beloved, reading, good sleep hygiene and tango.

A way I've found to nourish my spirit at home is to view a live-feed of a nesting eagle or other forest scene on YouTube. I'll keep it open on a browser tab as I work so that I can hear the forest sounds.

I take a renewal day in nature every month. This is a day for me to just be. The only agenda is to have no agenda and only do what moves me. I reconnect more firmly to what feeds my spirit during these days. It doesn't usually look like me sitting on a meditation cushion. More often than not it involves a solo run or hike and finding a place to just be and observe.

You, yourself deserve your love and compassion
more than anyone else. ~ Buddha

I take a long weekend at least four times a year to unplug and spiritually rejuvenate. During these longer renewals I get deeper in touch with what I love and reflect on how I can be more aligned with my joy.

Plan segments of inactivity and renewal activity for yourself. How deep you go with self-care / renewal has a direct bearing on how powerfully you can show up in a grounded state for your life.

Personal Journaling Exercise
Where have I made my self-care negotiable?
What would I stop doing if I was committed to better self-care?
Where can I make improvements in my self-care?
I commit to regular self-care in the form of...

The answer to overwhelm is not doing more, it's doing the few things that can move the needle in the right direction. A personal priority hierarchy allows for using your time in the best way. Tim Ferriss says, *"If you have more than three priorities, then you don't have any."*

The person to whom all activity and options are equally important can be maddening to be around. If you don't prioritize, everything can seem urgent and important. Living one's priorities that are in alignment with one's values is a wonderful place to be. Lived priorities are a form of self-care. Remember, *action will lead to insight more reliably than insight will lead to action.*

Take care of what's essential early in the day. Consider this as an investment to make the rest of your day function better. I pre-decide one to three main objectives for each day and if there is still energy after accomplishing those, I am free to add more (or not). I have a cutoff time when whatever is undone will have to be attended to another day.

Figure out what you need, put that in place, and remove what interferes with it. A complementary tactic is to get your most important things done by noon. This practice alone can be a game-changer.

Win the morning and you win the day. ~ Jim Rohn

Saying No

"*No*" can be a positive and empowering word. Saying, "*No*" is part of healthy boundary-setting. In Marshall Rosenburg's teaching of Non-Violent Communication (NVC) we learn that a, "*No*" to you is a, "*Yes*" to me. Saying, "*No*" can be a gift that you give other people. A real, "*No*" means that others can trust that when a, "*Yes*" comes, it is real.

What we don't do opens space for what we can do. **Not-To-Do** decisions are often better than To-Do lists. "*No*" to an energy drain is a, "*yes*" to filling yourself with what feeds you. As an example, I no longer answer phone calls from unrecognized numbers. This one decision frees me from a mini-decision each time that type of call comes in.

Soul Statement Examples

My boundaries are valid.
I prefer my real, but messy expression over the polished version.
Saying, "No" is a tool in service of my value and values.

Ask what you have to say, "*No*" to in order support better your self-care. Determine which activities don't serve your highest values and put them on a **Not-To-Do** list.

A Not-To-Do list might include:
I won't let people carry on too long about problems that
do not concern me.
I won't sleep in past 7am any longer.
I won't put off my exercise workout.
I won't surf the internet during my most productive hours.
I won't eat food with added sugar.
I won't look at electronic screens after 8pm.

What small thing would make a difference if you stopped doing it? Do you really enjoy mowing the lawn or are you spending precious weekend time to save a few bucks? A too-common example is, devoting your most productive hours to social media scrolling when you don't need to. I've been guilty of this in the past, but am very strict on this point now.

Personal Journaling Exercise
What is the best use of my free time?
What mundane tasks could be delegated or farmed out?
Am I saying, "No" to that which doesn't serve my
highest purpose?
What small thing would make a difference in my quality
of life if I stopped doing it?
My personal Not-To-Do list contains...

Yes, AND...

Saying, "*No*" skillfully is a skill. One of my favorite methods of saying, "*No*" is using, "*Yes, AND...*". Using, "*Yes, AND...*" can help move you away from being the nice doormat. In this way, you can assert your needs and not be an insensitive clod. For the next week, see if you can avoid using a simple, "*Yes*". This may sound like, "*I would like that AND it would work better for me if we did it this way...*".

Ideally, you would say, "*No*" when there isn't an enthusiastic "*Yes.*" The goal is to acknowledge desires and to decline (or modify) participation with grace. Accepting other people's proposals without modification in the interest of being a nice guy or nice gal turns down the volume of your interest. Consider that your partner doesn't need to be protected from your wants. They may just prefer the real version of you over the polished version!

Yes AND... Examples

"Yes, that sounds good AND I have a schedule conflict."
"That is interesting AND I won't be able to participate."
"What you suggest sounds great AND I would be able to
say "Yes" to an earlier start."

Notice what lights you up and what turns you down as you go through your day. Be present, but not self-absorbed. Much like driving a car while keeping your eye on the gauges, the juice in your emotional 'gas tank' is a way to monitor different parts of your spirit and welfare.

Pay attention to these signals and skillfully use, "*No*" or, "*Yes AND...*" in service of balance and focus. Speak to your needs and what you are able to offer using simple, kind and true language.

Soul Statement Examples

How I show up for myself is a valid purpose.
Saying "Yes" to life is attractive.

Cultivating Your Spirit

Time spent meditating and cultivating your spirit is never lost. When you let your mind rest in a resourced state it is natural to feel powerful, connected and unconcerned with income or outcome. This is an emanating and attracting vibration. Actions from this place are extra potent.

Soul Statement Examples

My inner stillness is available.
My inner stillness is my support.

Our lives are lived a micro-moment at a time. If we miss any moment, that particular grain of time has dropped through the center of a virtual hourglass and it's not coming back.

Personally, I want to be as present as I can for all of it. Just as the tallest buildings have the deepest foundations, our moments spent in stillness and quiet are part of strengthening a robust personal foundation.

Have your meditation modality be one that you respond to readily and joyfully. This way you will make time for it. I cannot stress this point enough, if you enjoy it, you'll keep returning to it. For example, many people make their daily run a meditative practice. The following meditation is one I enjoy for bringing me more energy and clarity.

Inner Glow Meditation

Sit comfortably and breathe in an easy, natural rhythm. Roll your shoulders, stretch, breath, sigh or yawn as needed to create more ease. You may turn on pleasing music if there are other sounds nearby. Close your eyes and visualize your breath as light entering your lungs.

With each inhalation, imagine light expanding out from your chest and filling your body. Notice how each and every one of your cells are turning on, like little lamps. Feel the newly lit up cells vibrate with happiness. Allow this light to infuse each organ of your body.

Feel your inner glow as ultimately attractive. You may visualize your desires in the form of imaginary moths that are drawn to your glowing self.

External Reminders

I love the tool of external reminders. The author and speaker, Mel Robbins, suggests setting self-soothe alarms on your phone. When the alarm sounds, remind yourself that you are enough and are sufficiently resourced.

Alarms to stop and feel can be set on the hour or just prior to arriving at work or going into a meeting or when you are about to arrive home. You may create a Soul Statement pop-up on your phone screen such as, "*I am loved.*" These messages will remind you to feel the best parts of you right then.

Internal Reminders

With consistent re-alignment, a new habit folds into the continuum of how you operate. A Soul Statement reminder is not just another thought among the din, but a call from your spirit to pause and remember what is true and right and important. Remember, **STOP** (press pause), **DROP** (go inside) and **ROLL** (with what shows up).

Soul Statement Example

My inner self knows what to do.

Emotional Home

Your emotional home is the feeling state in which you spend the most time. This is your default emotional status, all things being equal. Some emotional home examples are: Pessimism, Optimism, Cheerful Interest, Exuberance, Anxious, Concerned, Contentment, Ease and Wonder.

You can upgrade your emotional home by practicing self-acceptance and making time to find a place of contentment and belonging within. Contentment doesn't imply perfect, it's just that you are okay right now. Let the Soul Statement of, *"I am enough in this moment."* create a feeling pathway to where you want to be. Aim for a sure, neutral knowing without positive or negative judgment. Why not accept a bit of peace for a while?

Personal Journaling Exercise

Where do I return to emotionally when under stress or worry?
What would I name this default place?
What emotion do I want to spend more time feeling?

Emotional Home Meditation

Find a comfortable position for your body. Close your eyes and adjust your posture. Roll your shoulders, stretch, breath, sigh or yawn as needed to create more physical ease.

Feel an energetic grounding cord that goes from your hips to deep within the Earth. Imagine this cord like the root of a tree or a pillar of golden light. Notice how gravity holds you where you sit.

Allow your breath to find a natural rhythm. Allow your breath to soften and relax your body. Feel sacred breath animating your core. Take a few more breaths to feel beneath and beyond thinking. Focus on just being.

Now, let yourself be flooded with the emotion of home. Feel you heart awash in this secure feeling. This emotional home is the place inside where everything is okay. Feel your contented essence. Know that joy is your birthright.

Feel beyond thought and into the rightness of your essence. As you rest in this serene state, ask your heart for a message or symbol.

Aspects of You

We all have many sides (aspects) to who we are as a person. Some aspect examples are: the young child, the teenager, the young adult, the parent, the people-pleaser, the bread-winner, the competitor, the worried me, your present persona. You have a part of you that exhibits excellence, depth or ease.

Other parts of you may sometimes feel discouraged, anxious or even helpless. We all have habits or transient personas that we wish were more empowered. We all have aspects that are worthy of respect that we want to express more frequently.

The more you're aware of what's alive inside, the better you can express your needs with skill, grace and respect. Naming a given aspect allows for a bit of emotional distance from that part of your makeup.

My unsure, fearful child is named *Boy-Small*. I can still honor *Boy-Small* when I call forth *Warrior-Committed*. Those two parts can both be present at the same time. One can express concerns and the other can provide compassion, protection and direction.

Other examples of powerful names are, *Deep-Heart*, *Tree-Grounded* and *Rock-Capable*. When you want to bring a more empowered version of yourself to a given situation, declare a Soul Statement like, **"*I'm Heart-Warrior*"** or, **"*I'm Energy-Flow and I bring light forth.*"** A sure-voiced, **"*I got this*"** and a power gesture can anchor you to a desired aspect then and there.

Archetype Examples
King or Queen with easy, flowing lifestyle
Neo freeing his mind (from *The Matrix* movie)
Warrior fighting for freedom and family (William Wallace,
Robert the Bruce, Joan of Arc, Cochise or Osceola)

By really feeling your power aspect, you're re-training your nervous system and your mind. With practice, you can more and more easily call up relevant energy in order to counteract an unhelpful state. You can more and more easily anchor to a profound part of your nature in a moment.

Soul Statement Examples
I trust my Inner King.
I serve my Inner Queen.

Chapter Summary
There is the truth of who you are and the rest is just story. When you're in touch with your truth, you can be present for life. Soul Statements help bring you there. What's right in any given moment is always there to be recognized and claimed.

Fresh insight should, ideally, lead to improved actions or

behavior. New and better actions should serve greater insight as a positive feedback loop.

Your emotional state will determine your activity and choices. Upgrade your emotional home as needed. Inhabit the part of you that exhibits excellence, depth or ease. When you are clear on the inside you can speak your truth more simply and with kindness.

Why not act as your own best friend (with compassion and patience)? Shrink internal sarcasm and belittling. Remember that you are capable, brave, resourced, smart, spiritual... Persist in the practice of focusing on your deepest, most relevant value.

Make certain that you have the right priorities. Say, "*No*" in service of balance and focus. Use, "*Yes, AND...*" in the service of your self-care and priorities. Put the most resourced version of you in charge.

When you find you, you'll know because it feels like you've arrived home. Your heart will bring you there if you allow it to guide you. Use external and internal reminders as needed.

Plan segments of inactivity and renewal activity for yourself. Sustain intimacy with yourself with journaling.

In the next chapter, we'll address how to find your certainty and ease. We'll speak to living a bigger version of you while keeping it light. There will be a section about the usefulness of a complaint fast and a blessing practice, in addition to **Spirit Vows** and the importance of monitoring **Spirit Vital signs**.

If you are moved to, tag me in a social media post, describing your up-leveled self-talk and/or what you are committed to stopping (from your Not-To list), with the hashtags #selftalk #committed

6

GIVER OF POWER

The way I find more of myself is to silence out the world.
~ David Goggins

Soul Statements help you remain aware of your true home and your essence. When you know who and what you are, your power naturally turns up. This makes it easier to live as the truest version of you. Increased serenity comes from living as who you were born to be.

Soul Statement Example
I have a power place within.

In his book, *Artic Dreams*, Barry Lopez writes about how the northernmost Inuit people's name for the polar bear translates as, *Giver of Power.* As Barry Lopez tells it, if a lone hunter is confronted by a polar bear with nowhere to escape (only flat ice in every direction) and he lives to tell the tale, he inevitably uncovers a deeper part of himself in those moments with the bear. This is a portion of his essence that he did not have access to before, but which he can now incorporate into his life, hence the name, *Giver of Power*.

Coming face-to-face with a serious cancer diagnosis and years-long treatment has been my *Giver of Power*. I got to feel into who I am beyond fear and desire. I had to decide how hard I was willing to fight for life and why. I continue to review and update what I believe about myself in order to be fully engaged in the fight for my life.

Soul Statement Examples

Health is my birthright.
Love washes through every part of me.

Fear waits to pounce from ambush when I am most vulnerable. Fear stalks me like a silent wolf at the perimeter of an ancient campfire. Fear wells up in my chest and informs me when I am focusing in a poor direction. It sometimes tries to enter my dreams and my quiet moments. The aggressive treatment of cancer is its own challenge with unexpected blows to roll with and losses to grieve.

For every loss along the way I could remain in sorrow or choose to focus on what I was gaining in exchange. Focusing on my gains was an absolute game-changer for me. It moved me from self-pity to clarity about why I was in the battle. There were more lessons on this voyage back to well-being that I could not know all at once. This journey was a slow-motion marathon.

The texture and layers of pain have their own purity and their own teachings. There was no short-cutting or getting around the predictable grief and sorrow, but I could not afford to spiral down too far into morbid reflection. The hurdles that I had to clear in this period of time were a stark example of the powerful adage: *The way out is through.*

I am happy for what I can do. This illness helped me stop doing things that weren't the best use of my time. When the amount of time one has left might be drastically shortened, simple decisions become stark. *"Is X or Y activity serving my highest value?"* and *"What if I didn't do this thing?"* These are natural questions when considering onrushing mortality. These questions are useful for any of us, anytime.

Soul Statement Example

I'm stronger than my challenges.

The Best Day of My Life

One thing that living with cancer has done is increase my everyday appreciation. When the potential for no more days becomes a much-too-real outcome, each day is precious. I may not be having an ideal day, but I am in it with a reasonable expectation of another day to live after this one. I hold the awareness that this very day I'm inhabiting is the best day of my life. Every day.

Other days may have held more pleasure, excitement, closeness, joy or accomplishment. There have been days in my life that were filled with wonder, adventure or more ease and connectedness than today. **This day stands as the best simply because I am living it now.**

All previous days, whether amazing or difficult, have passed into memory. They are encoded in my cells and psyche and they led me directly to here. Each one of them informs my present. And it is the present day that matters most.

Today is what I can experience and that makes it the best of all. All future days haven't arrived and when they do (God-willing) I will experience them one at a time in real time. Every future day, when I'm living it, will be the new best day of my life.

Don't make light of suffering, but find light in suffering.
~ Quan Yin

A simple life is a good thing. Today is not a rehearsal for tomorrow. This moment is all; I can touch it and taste it. I've had to do some difficult tasks, which were made easier by realizing that I hold the prize. **The prize is an embodied, compassionate, aware life**. Triumph and disaster are imposters. (Thank you, Rudyard Kipling). External accomplishment and attachment to external circumstance are both traps and neither define me.

Whether feeling high or low, each is just a moment. Every experience gives way to another. Recognize the sacredness of each moment. The blessing of life is enough. Just being present is enough. When you find yourself centered in the moment, you win. If I were in the commandment-writing business I'd inscribe one as: **Be Thou Here**.

Re-claiming one's personal power is a natural outcome for many of my coaching clients. Personal power is supported by the practice of speaking directly to one's needs in a timely fashion. Each of us can access a reservoir of source energy and inspiration that is 'the deep within'. We can each be our own *Giver of Power*. As I write this, I was born 59 years ago. This is Corey version 5.9 and the present is perfect because I say so.

Personal Journaling Exercise
My own Giver of Power has been...
My challenges have produced gifts for me as follows...

Hoka Hey!

In the Native American Sun Dance tradition there is a term, *"Hoka Hey!"* This basically translates as, *"Let's go. Today is a good day to die!"*. This refers to giving the best of oneself and not holding back or waiting for a better day. That way if death comes today, life was lived to its fullest and all was given. Everything that we had has been left on the field. *"Hoka Hey!"* is a call to live into one's full potential. Right now. There is no better day than this one.

Spirit Vows

I coined the term, **Spirit Vow**, for an ironclad agreement that you make with your inner self. You may find it helpful to declare a solemn **Spirit Vow** to no longer consciously abandon yourself. Self-abandonment occurs by compromising or negotiating one's values to gain favor or save face in the eyes of other people.

Spirit Vow Examples

I vow to hold my heart as sacred and worthy of protection.
I vow to never turn away from what I value most dearly.
I vow to speak up for my needs even when I'm
uncomfortable doing so.
I will never abandon you. (Speak this to your own heart.)
I take you to be my body in this life and to treat you with
care and respect.
I vow to choose compassion and kindness in the face of
adversity or challenge.
I vow to show compassion and consideration to myself
as my own best friend.

Putting your **Spirit Vows** on paper helps you to incorporate supportive practices when faced with the choice of holding to your values or not. Reviewing **Spirit Vows** help you notice where you may have fallen back into the habit of internal compromise. Have your outer actions match your inner values. This congruency can be a guide to more freely serve all of life.

Shrinking your presence or subsuming your values to make others feel safer is generally a poor strategy. Doing so is a form of self-abandonment. Whom does it serve to play small? The answer is: *No one.* When does it serve to turn joy or power down on the inside? The answer is: *Not really ever.*

When you diminish your desires, the world says, *"Okay got it, here is your self-worth reflected back to you."* You are cheating yourself when you act and feel less than what you're capable of. Returning to alignment with that which feeds your spirit will re-orient you to your power.

Soul Statement Examples
I am as important as anybody.
I have a lot to create and to give.

Having personal **Spirit Vows** helps one remain connected to what's most important. Honoring **Spirit Vows** leads to becoming a more integrated and potent human being. This isn't a license to share one's innermost thoughts to any persons who will listen.

I think of honoring a **Spirit Vow** during a moment of choice as *Breaking Deep.* Folding or ignoring one's values in the moment could be called *Breaking Small.* Just feel who you are, quietly repeat a **Spirit Vow**, and offer grounded, secure presence.

Personal Journaling Exercise
Ways that I abandoned myself at times were...
A time that I've negotiated on my value was...
A personal Spirit Vow for me is...

Body Wisdom

It is often useful to check in with your body's wisdom. Does a sensation occur in a specific part of your body when you pose a given question? Sometimes a person may feel a whole-body excitement or a whole-body numbness. When that happens, it tends to be a very certain sign.

My coaching clients will often place a hand over their navel and feel for heaviness or lightness there. The way I operate, a body signal of *"Yes"* equals Go. A whole-body *"Yes"* equals Go Bigger. A *"No"* equates to find a different door or direction. A whole-body *"No"* signals to exit quickly and definitively.

Surface thoughts will often offer resistance, causing you to second-guess your own clarity. Acknowledge any doubt or self-evaluation and know that you have deeper certainty underneath your thoughts.

Tune in to your heart or other power center and ask, *"Does this thought bring me a feeling of relaxation or tension?"* Another useful question is, *"Do I feel lighter or heavier in my body when I have this thought?"* Your body doesn't play games. In my experience, the body knows what is best.

Soul Statement Example

My body is able to say, "Yes" and "No."

Trust Your Certainty

Years ago, a friend and I descended partway down a high cliff in the desert to climb back up to the top (just for fun). It was a fine plan until the rope became stuck far above us during our descent and we found ourselves trapped on a small ledge. We were 100 feet below the top of the cliff rim and 200 feet above the rocky talus slope below. The rope was not long enough for us to rappel down to the base of the cliff.

Luckily, I had recently learned (in practice) how to ascend a fixed rope using two small cords (prusiking) and I had two small cords with me. Because the upper portion of the cliff overhung our ledge, to begin my ascent I had to fully trust the integrity of the cords on the rope and commit to a 'king swing' out over the deep canyon.

There would be no second chance, the cords and the rope would either hold or not. Once I had made the swing I'd be dangling in space, and would not be able to return to the ledge. I would have to get through the initial fear and then begin the exhausting effort of inching my way up 100 feet of rope.

Another choice was to wait for someone to eventually discover us. It was now Sunday afternoon in a remote part of the New Mexico, so we might not be discovered until the following weekend. Without water to drink in that environment for a week, a body-retrieval would be the result (as we'd be too far gone to rescue).

I made an intuitive soul-searching. I felt into my center and connected to a certainty that I could safely get to the top of the cliff. I inwardly said to myself, "I can do this" and then I acted. I made the knots, set my feet in the cord loops, checked the knots again and swung outward and away from the semi-secure ledge.

Now I was hanging in the air like a spider on a thread. I felt vulnerable by not being able to reach back to the cliff, but was now irrevocably committed. Fear began to well up in my throat. I metaphorically put the fear in my back pocket and focused on each move or the slow and sustained effort upward.

Once I was finally on level ground, I re-configured the rope to protect my companion as he climbed up the rock face. At a minimum, a cold night on that small ledge without warm clothes, food or water would have been a tenuous place to be. But, if I had not felt my certainty, I would not have attempted this self-rescue.

Soul Statement Example
I have a certainty that is deeper than my thoughts.

Being in Your Ease

By remaining grounded it is easier to be present for life as it is occurring. From a grounded state you may find yourself naturally and appropriately containing your energy. You'll then be able to more skillfully communicate what moves and interests you (and what doesn't). With practice, it becomes easier to say what you're up for and what you're not up for. This is called, *being in your ease.*

Soul Statement Examples

I can access my center.
My groundedness allows for increased sureness.

The first time I used a shovel my grandfather instructed me to not grip the handle too tightly. I only understood after blisters formed on my hands. Likewise, holding emotions or setbacks more lightly allows for a bit of perspective. Holding yourself and everything that occurs in your life with more ease is not theoretical. Loosen your grip. Allow space for life to unfold in its own time.

> *Learn to do everything lightly. Yes, feel lightly*
> *even though you're feeling deeply.* ~ Aldous Huxley

Hold awareness of who and what you are lightly. Going deep does not imply (and is not an excuse for) being overly serious. One doesn't need to overtly emphasize depth in every conversation. Doing so can lead to listener burnout. When you're feeling centered and complete, you don't need to use a given interaction to excavate a bigger truth. It is enough to simply be interested in the person whom you're with.

Soul Statement Example
As I my serenity increases, I can hold circumstance more lightly.

You don't want to be the person that goes around asking super-serious questions and nothing else. The person that only talks about deep issues becomes a self-centered bore. These folks can veer into Winston Churchill's definition of a fanatic, which is, "*Someone who can't change their mind and won't change the subject*". Speaking from deep, as it were, may simply be expressed by living with calm, contained energy.

Personal Journaling Exercise
Write at least 30 answers for each of the following prompts.

The deep me values…

The deep me wants…

My commitment to listening for my body's wisdom is…

Re-visit your answers in six months.

Complaint Fast
Doing a *complaint fast* is a simple as inserting an appreciation in place of every emerging complaint. It is a form of override that keeps a person going in a good direction. If this is difficult for you, it likely means that it's a good thing to get better at.

To become a better partner, be a better *emotional container* rather than talking about every little bump in the road of life. Even when you're not doing a *complaint fast* perfectly, there is still benefit from the awareness and the attempt.

The *complaint fast* mostly takes place inside your own head. Not complaining does not prohibit you from expressing needs. The idea is to simply bypass complaining and go directly to solution-finding. This may involve a request, changing one's own behavior or exiting a situation. Making requests of other people is a key strategy for getting one's needs met.

Soul Statement Examples
I am not what I complain about.
The grounded version of me is always accessible.

The only real barrier to consistent practice of a complaint fast is ego and forgetting. A friend of mine, says, *"God Bless It!"* when he is shocked or experiences something potentially upsetting. I appreciate being around him for these reminders of emphasizing blessing over complaint.

I carry a card in my wallet that says, **Notice the Best Part**. This is my reminder to look for good in everything. Let a new paradigm of blessing become who you are and watch your experience of life change. Can you challenge yourself to maintain a Blessing Practice for a week or a month?

Blessing Practice
Look for what is right and bless everything you see for 24 hours.
Pro version: Start the 24-hours over each time you utter or
think a complaint.

Mindfulness
The rushing or worried you is always available, but the grounded you is always accessible. Slowing down helps gain internal perspective to foster greater inner and outer harmony. If we were to believe EVERY thought, we could not function. A self-aware mind helps one choose which thoughts to invite in for virtual tea or coffee.

Mindful awareness IS the goal. Mindful awareness isn't something we get. It is something we incubate and create the conditions for. As mindfulness becomes more familiar and natural, you can keep a measure of it even while running from task to task.

Many of us have a default habit of just wanting to get to the next moment. The way to interrupt that pattern is through a regular practice of returning one's attention to the present moment. In his book, *Wise Mind Open Mind*, Ronald A. Alexander, Ph.D. advises, *"Simply be still and watch your breath."*

You can be high on your own supply. ~ Wim Hof

Ongoing quiet reflection helps one enjoy the present and it is a key component of self-care. To put attention on the breath, just breathe naturally and observe the in and out flow of air from your lungs. Allow internal noise to settle out. Gently keep your attention on the simple process of breathing.

In his book, *Joy On Demand*, Chade-meng Tan gives a superb explanation of putting all your attention perfectly on one breath. He instructs the reader to then do one more breath in the same way. And so on. The important thing is to keep bringing your complete attention back to the current breath.

Meditation doesn't have to always be sitting still with your eyes closed. Walking or running in nature is meditation for many people. I love rock-climbing for the one-pointed concentration it demands. I also love kirtan (devotional chanting) as a way to drop into a meditative zone with community. Do whatever is enjoyable for you to achieve a relaxed state of mind. **Hint:** If it is enjoyable, you'll be likely to do it more often.

The meditation teacher, Sam Harris, describes the concept of repetitions (reps). By this he means simply returning again and again to your practice when you have drifted away. The idea is that doing these 'reps' builds your meditation muscle.

Another amazing meditation practice is resonant brain entrainment, which gently brings a person into deeper brainwave states. Quite simply, a soundtrack plays soothing music under which a different subliminal tone is presented to each ear. This stimulates the brain to reconcile the tones and build coherence. My favorite resonant brain entrainment program is iAwake and I use a soft headband with embedded speakers (SleepPhones™).

Personal Journaling Exercise
When have I felt most connected to my center?
What brings me to this state?

Quiet reflection helps you grow in an intentional direction and stay in alignment with what's important. This can be as simple as sitting quietly and contemplating what is true for you. Your gut (or another wise part of the body) can guide you. The more you listen for the messages of your body, the more you will hear them.

When you reliably rest in stillness, you have more to offer the world. Consider incorporating a quiet time in the morning to be a *meeting with you*. A '**Morning Me**', if you will.

Until you make the unconscious conscious, it will
direct your life and you will call it fate. ~ Carl Gustav Jung

Your mind is not always the best judge of how to budget your life's energy. Let your nervous system have a vote as to whether you're living into your highest expression or not. When you don't know what to do, consider the option of doing absolutely nothing for a time. Sitting in stillness is a way to visit the deeper knowing that lives in your body.

When you're connected to your deeper self, true knowing and inspiration will bubble up to the surface. Wait to do a given thing until it feels like a direct impulse from your soul. Don't just do something, sit and feel. Truth lives in your cells. Your body vibrates in present time.

Soul Statement Examples
Inspiration from my spirit bubbles up when I am still and quiet.
Stillness calms and aligns me.

The external world is not going to hand you power or purpose. You must feel it within and then decide how to express it. Your soul is where your creativity and genius originates. This genius of which I speak goes beyond making a difference. It is using your unique skills and sensitivities to meaningfully contribute to the world.

Personal Journaling Exercise
What's not true about me is...
What I believe about me is...
Are my actions and behaviors congruent with what I believe about me?

Source Meditation
Sit in a quiet place and find a comfortable position. Make micro-adjustments as needed (yawn, stretch, roll your shoulders...). Close your eyes and allow your breath to find a natural rhythm.

Your cells have encoded with a template of health and your soul's priorities. Feel your cells lighting up as you bring in Source energy (in the form of golden light) with each inhalation. Allow Source energy to fill you from toes to crown.

Feel for sensations or messages in various areas of your body. Contemplate what's true about you. Connect to the part of you that knows what to do.

Take a few breaths to drop down beneath and beyond words. Feel the peaceful knowing that exists in silence. Feel the importance of being in truth. Rest in this place.

Spirit Vital Signs

There are many internal cues for when it's a good time to tune up. I call these **Spirit Vital Signs** or **Spirit Vitals**. They are as relevant as blood pressure and heart rate. My primary **Spirit Vital** is my voice. When I'm rushing, distracted or upset my voice tone rises and the tempo increases. I tend to sound more immature and less grounded at these times.

Another **Spirit Vital** may be feeling edgy. This can present as snappish and indicates that you may have let your self-care commitment slip. A more subtle **Spirit Vital** is connection or disconnection to what is alive in your body.

When disconnection occurs, a person may be living in their head or simply engrossed in a project and their body feels blank. One may be going through the motions of getting something done. If someone asked them what they're feeling while in that state they'd likely be at a loss to answer unless first slowing down to feel.

To discover your own **Spirit Vitals**, think of times when you've felt *off*. This can look like stress, impatience or occupied with worry. Perhaps you find yourself thinking that another person is the cause of a current upset? If you feel jammed for time and are rushing around, that may be another clue that you've wandered off center.

Personal Journaling Exercise

My personal Spirit Vitals are...

Ignoring Oneself

Life has a way of sending us invitations to wake up. In the early 1990's I was the field director of a wilderness-based drug and alcohol recovery program and I poured so much into the duties that I wasn't getting enough food or rest. I remember eating an apple and wondering when I had eaten last. All I knew was that it definitely wasn't yesterday or the day before that.

The least problem got me very upset. I deferred all personal issues to an undefined later date. I knew I was losing weight, but I had no idea that I had gotten down to 110 pounds before I physically collapsed. Luckily, most people aren't near as dense as I was then. I share this story to illustrate how bad it can get when we ignore our internal voice.

Soul Statement Example

My Spirit Vital signs are important signals.

Stalking Your Shadow

Don't hide your motivation for a given action underneath a story that you tell yourself. Don Miguel Ruiz, Baba Dez Nichols and other teachers talk about the benefits of *stalking your shadow*.

We stalk our shadow by rigorously telling ourselves the truth on the inside about our actions and motivations. Truth-avoidance can be a challenging habit to break, but the benefits are great. Discomfort is not a cue to run away or rush to fix feelings. Allow discomfort to show you where your motivation or actions were self-serving or less-than-honorable. Cultivate fearlessness in this way and your life will change.

Soul Statement Example
My shadow is a valuable teacher.

Stalking one's shadow can be as light as you wish to make it. This stalking occurs on the inside as you practice rigorous honesty with your motivations for any given action. Inner honesty is the key that unlocks the door to a greater life.

Personal Journaling Exercise
What was my motivation for a given action (or non-action)?
What is the clear request of my heart?
How can I 'keep it light', while expressing my needs?

Childhood fears become adult beliefs. Your current experience is a reflection of what you already believe. It is right and important to update childhood beliefs as an adult. When you realize that your current story is unhelpful, interrupt yourself and return to congruency by stating (inwardly or outwardly) a true and positive Soul Statement that replaces the newly discarded thought.

Decide what is actually true, then insert that as the dominant feeling. For example, *"My old story was X, but my real belief is Y."* A powerful truth is now embedded to counter and supplant the outdated story.

When I believe my thoughts, I suffer. ~ Byron Katie

Personal Journaling Exercise
What do I still believe from childhood that hasn't been updated?
What has been the benefit to me of keeping X behavior?
Has X behavior been worth the cost?

Circumstances are a constant invitation to make a powerful or weak choice. Use the useful internal questions, "*What is my highest desire? Do I want to continue this activity or extract myself or modify my participation?*"

Using self-inquiry at this time can be like a dial-up to spirit to lend perspective on the larger purpose that the activity may or may not serve. You may replace non-useful questions by asking simple, powerful questions. When you take a stand for love and presence you create a better reality.

Uncovering Primary Emotion
(Journal or speak the following when you're upset.)

I mad about X and what am I actually afraid of is...

I'm angry because Y and, actually I'm needing...

Vision Questing
For many years I guided people through vision quest experiences. This involved four days and three nights inside a 10-foot circle while fasting, praying and looking within. There is simply nothing to do. There is just you. Utter boredom is part of the design. The boredom barrier must be fought through in order to access the reward that is your deep wisdom.

Soul Statement Example
My old stories are just stories.

The plan is to let the mind run through every mundane, profane and boring thought along with one's angst and worry until it exhausts itself. The challenge is to sit with one's angst and worry and not run or shrink from fears and doubts. This is the time to go under the surface distraction. A person's essence that lives underneath all of this is their treasure.

When the mind finally pauses, deeper insight bubbles up. If the pure message from your soul lasts for two minutes, the entire four days was worthwhile. The bigger you that dwells within is waiting for you to dive under the surface of your mind and claim your birthright.

> *The most important day of your life is the day you were born.*
> *The second most important day is when you find out why.*
> *~ Mark Twain*

I went on my first vision quest at age 17. There was no pen and paper. No phone. No food. No fire. No shelter. No place to explore. There was nothing to occupy my time except thinking and observing nature (which wasn't moving very quickly).

I became bored beyond description. I became weary of my mundane and repetitive thoughts. I prayed. On day three, I danced until I was physically exhausted.

The only emotion I felt on day four was disappointment. I had no notable dreams or vision. No revelation or insight had occurred for me. As I prepared to leave, I resigned myself to this having been a fruitless effort. Then, an epiphany snuck up on me. It waited until I wasn't looking.

For a few minutes I felt a sure knowing that I was a worthy man and that my life was to be an example for others. Living honorably was my contribution. Those four days were invaluable as they got me to that holy moment.

I walked out and rejoined my community. The light in the pines had a special clarity. Every object seemed closer than before. The world was the same one I'd left, but I was now connected to a powerful piece of me and was seeing with enhanced vision.

The world encourages us to live in our head. Luckily, we don't need four days of fasting to contact inner wisdom. When you go inside and touch your truth, you can discover profound and unshakeable knowing.

Powerful insight often comes fully-formed as an epiphany in an instant. The whisper of spirit is often literally a whisper. It behooves each of us to get quiet and ask (then listen) for a message from our spirit or from the Greater Spirit.

Personal Journaling Exercise

What feeling is alive in my body and what would help me now?

How can I ask for my highest desire in a simple and clear manner?

When the knowing of your soul is downloaded you say, *"Aha, I got it!"*. Soul power felt at the surface of your consciousness is an unmovable stand. When you get it, it is so. You may find yourself exclaiming, *"So shall it be done!"*.

Once you have this type of personal revelation, you aren't likely going to need a do-over soon. That being said, the work to stay on course with the message of your spirit is never done. One of my spiritual teachers is fond of saying, *"The reward for enlightenment is work."* In other words, once you know what you want to do in this world, your important work begins.

Chapter Summary

When you say, *"Yes"* to the power that is in each moment and stop living in an outdated story, life gets easier. Become aware that today is the best day of your life because you are living it now. Today is not a rehearsal for tomorrow. This moment is all.

Monitor your **Spirit Vitals**. Check in with your body's wisdom and trust your certainty.

Fast from complaining. Notice the best part and offer blessings.

Sharing your deepest self in every interaction is generally not needed or desirable. Staying light while feeling deep is a skill that improves with practice. It's easier to build connection when you limit your own sharing and simply listen.

The world needs each one of us if we are to create a happy future for all sentient beings with whom we share this exquisite home. **Remember**: *The task that hinders you is your task.*

In the next chapter, we'll discover how to recognize cultural ritual as an opportunity to skillfully speak the unspoken and deepen interaction with others. We will also demonstrate how making Soul Statements at daily transitions will up-level your interactions and experience. We'll also explore the power of forgiveness and amends.

If you are moved to, tag me in a social media post declaring your certainty and promises to yourself, with the hashtags #sayyes #promises

7

RITUAL AND FAMILY

Change my vibration and I change my results.
~ Bruce H. Lipton, Ph.D.

In both mundane and sacred ritual, a societal window of permission is open to speak to deeper values and true feelings. This is when we may hear what is normally left unsaid during regular life. Speaking in a deeper way is often an expectation at such times.

Soul Statement Example

I am connected to my heart.

Societal ritual is the time and place for heartfelt statements. Times of family crisis or transition have their own rituals —coming of age, a child leaving home or the passing of a loved one. Holidays and birthdays are other opportunities to speak more deeply to how we cherish one another.

Two other examples of times that are conducive to truth-telling are graduations and awards ceremonies. This is when we hear statements like, *"I'm proud of you"* and, *"You've done so well."* Heartfelt statements are a deep truth-telling regarding positive attributes or feelings for another person. This communication is a type of Soul Statement.

Soul Statement Examples

I am blessed beyond measure.
Love is at my center.

One Mother's Day, I wrote a letter to my mom describing what I appreciate about her and who she is for me. Composing this letter was a soul-searching exercise, as I had to reflect on who I have become. I noticed how many of my best character traits can be traced back to her influence. I also felt more deeply into how blessed I am to have been adopted and raised by her.

A nice ritual to do on Valentine's Day is to write a love note to a child or the children in your life in addition to your intimate partner. In this note, you may tell them what you appreciate and admire in them and perhaps what you wish for them.

This type of message could also go into a birthday card. Most of us could speak to deeper values and sentiments more frequently in regular life. For example, in our home, we say mealtime prayers out loud. We may also speak gratitude and appreciations at that time, too.

Personal Journaling Exercise

What family or societal rituals are most impactful to me?
What I could do to deepen the experience of these moments?

Consider creating a brief personal ritual that would consistently ground you into your core essence in the midst of daily life. Your personal ritual could be a simple hand-on-heart along with an inward Soul Statement like, "*I love you fiercely and will never abandon you.*" You may supercharge the impact by doing it while looking in a mirror.

You may ritualize most any activity. A popular one with my coaching clients, is an exercise workout. While lifting weights, you might hold a Soul Statement in your consciousness, such as, "*I'm strong. I'm made of tough stuff.*" On a treadmill you may internally repeat "*I'm doing this as an act of love to myself.*" A Soul Statement can serve as a reminder that this is when and how you shift into a more powerful state.

A personal ritual doesn't have to be longer than a minute or two, but it can *true-up* your spirit. Why wouldn't you want to live each day as a more integrated version of you? Increased integration allows you to better maintain internal clarity with why you act and speak the way you do.

Soul Statement Example
I'm doing this (self-care) as an act of love.

My success in a given week depends on certain non-negotiable rituals such as stretching, core-strengthening and meditation. I like the metaphor as weight-bearing exercise being a large boulder in the stream of my day that the water of other activities must flow around.

In order to create space for your critical self-care, figure out the important pieces and assemble or re-assemble your life around them. My time for exercise is after coffee and before breakfast. For my writing, I fuel up and then do a short grounding meditation to begin. My schedule prompt for writing literally states:

Meal - Meditate - Go.

My life is controlled by what I do consistently. ~ Tony Robbins

We all have self-care rituals such as showering, making breakfast, etc. Why not increase the intentionality and positive impact by incorporating a silent Soul Statement at those times? Rituals that you repeat over time will bring results.

When you make set times for self-care, it is more likely to happen. In the past, I've used either a day-timer or a document with checkboxes for each key self-care piece so that I can review how well I did at the end of the week. I would send this completed document on Monday morning to an accountability buddy and he would send me his.

Personal Journaling Exercise
What steps can I take to up-level my self-care?
Who might be my accountability buddy?

Sleep Transitions
The moments upon awaking from sleep are a good opportunity to listen to the wisdom of your body. We have an opportunity to feel our essential nature at the portal of sleep. Entering sleep and waking from sleep are holy moments. I usually meditate at this time. This is also an ideal time to feel gratitude in order to set a positive tone for the day.

Soul Statement Example
My dreams hold valuable understanding for me.

You can leverage the transition from sleep to waking by capturing the wisdom of the dream state. Dreams utilize the non-verbal language of symbology. Lessons from your deep well of knowing, that is available in dreams, can inform waking life. Recording your dreams as soon as you awaken is a way of honoring messages from spirit. Using a dream journal or voice recorder allows you to later share with a trusted friend or therapist, who may grasp what is not obvious to you.

Bedtime Ritual

Before sleep, set an intention to remember your dreams. You may request an answer or greater understanding for a specific issue. As you fall asleep. Imagine and intend that you are taking a virtual elevator to your inner being. Ask, *"Can my life get even better?"* Do this every evening for a couple weeks and notice what changes occur.

Posture Point Mini-Ritual

I have a sticky note upon which is written, **POSTURE**, on the doorframe of both my bedroom and my office. It's a notice to straighten up as I pass by. As I do so, my attention shifts to how I'm holding my body and I give my brain a Soul Statement to anchor into a more powerful emotional posture. In this way, I use the simple act of traversing a doorway as a shift point. When my posture lifts, my sense of self rises with it.

Dial up the feeling of you by bringing a little more of you to the room and to the moment. This is how you can up-level your presence a notch. It's so great that such a simple and doable action provides immediate benefit! Adding a Soul Statement with a quick power gesture brings even more of the essential you into the here and now. Don't think 'better', just go deeper!

What if you let people see the best version of you when you enter a room? How might your interactions change if you were to adjust your posture each time you pass through a doorway? Remember, as with most things, success is in the consistent doing.

Posture Point Soul Statements

I'm guided by my deep core.
There is strength in my center.
I'm where I need to be. Divine timing is at play.

My coaching clients find it very helpful to make normal daily shifts into **Posture Points**. For example, brushing your teeth or otherwise looking in a mirror can be a cue to up-level your emotional and physical posture. Grinding coffee, blending a smoothie and even sitting on the toilet can be prompts to un-slouch the back and raise your diaphragm. A favorite cue is when I step into the morning shower and I keep my best posture for the duration of the wash.

These activities have a built-in redundancy so utilize as many of them as you can. Make use of simple, everyday activities to create **Posture Points** as a way of increasing attention to how you hold yourself in a given moment.

Personal Journaling Exercise

A cue that I could employ to make a posture adjustment is...

Being Seen

A good aspiration is to love yourself as your soul loves you. If you're up for a challenge, spend a few minutes gazing at the bathroom mirror. This is a quick way to be seen. Offer your reflection love and compassion with your eyes and your heart. Look at yourself in the best light. Try and look at yourself the way God does. Extend forgiveness for your shortcomings.

In a very real sense, the world is your mirror. There is always a reciprocal on the inside for that which disturbs you on the outside. You can offer compassion to any particular part of you. Feel compassion and self-forgiveness as deeply as you can. The more you engage your heart, the more effective self-compassion practice will be.

If you're not relishing something about yourself, release attachment to it. This is not always easy. However deep you are able to feel during this practice, you will find a matching benefit. Perhaps you may include this Soul Statement, "*I love you just the way you are.*"

Being Seen Exercise

Stand in front of a mirror and look for your essence. Say, "*Hello*" to the genuine you. With your eyes, offer compassion and forgiveness to your reflection.

Speak a Soul Statement with as much feeling as you can muster. Say it again to make this Soul Statement a sure knowing. Some Soul Statements that my coaching clients have used are, "*I so love you*" and, "*I was born for a reason.*"

Up-Level Transitions

More than a few couples whom I've coached have up-leveled their daily transitions. They discuss ahead of time what their ideal coming or going exchange looks like. One person may like to hear a certain phrase. Another person may prefer warm, but silent eye contact.

Instead of a "*hello*" from another room, it is honoring to pause other activity to say go over and say, "*hello*" with eye contact and a warm kiss when your partner arrives. The important thing is to be really present with each other, even for brief moments.

Too often we hesitate to speak true feelings of love. When we don't use our voice in the moment, the moment goes on by. Why not take another ten seconds at everyday transitions to offer extra kindness to a loved one? When you do, both lives are made richer. Sharing what is meaningful increases meaning in life.

The only time I recall telling my adoptive dad, "I love you" is the day I left home at age 18. Finally, there was no other thing left to pack or do, but to say goodbye. I told him that I was leaving and we just stood awkwardly. Then I stepped forward and hugged him.

When we embraced, I felt heartache welling up of not being as close to him for those last few years as I wished I had been. I felt his devotion of working every day to provide for me, my sister and mom. I wanted to say thank you for all of it and how much I appreciated him for giving his life for us. All I could do was say, "I love you Dad."

I saw tears in his eyes as I stepped back. I walked to my car and drove away. Even though I was unable to say all of what he was to me, just summing it up with "I love you" was a giant leap for me. I will be forever glad that I spoke those words out loud, because he unexpectedly passed away three weeks later.

Forgiveness

Forgiveness is a spiritual discipline that lets you reclaim your spirit. The author, Caroline Myss, says, *"Unforgiveness is a message to the universe that I want to repeat this experience."*

My life changed drastically for the better when I began practicing another bit of advice from her, which is, *"Harbor no thought that will burn."* An incredibly useful ritual is to formally forgive oneself for poor behavior, due to operating from false beliefs and fears in the past.

Soul Statement Example

Empowered delight is the vibration of my cells.

Making confessions and amends is a form of spiritual cleansing. Catholics and members of 12-Step programs are on to something as telling God and another human being the exact nature of your wrongs (along with appropriate amends) leads to feeling clean and free.

The saying, "*We're only as sick as our secrets*", is so very true. Shame locks away a portion of our power. When we feel clean, we naturally want to continue feeling clean. This leads a person to remain in integrity by making better choices.

You are perfect exactly as you are; there is no need to change anything except the thoughts that you aren't good enough.
~ Byron Katie

Amends

There is great benefit by being honest about one's behavior and making amends when needed. If you wish to fully claim your personal power and place in this world, there are few things more powerful than the ritual of making amends with self.

When a person tells the truth on the inside and makes an appropriate '*mending*' they become more integrated. Integrating these spirit pieces helps us live from a higher and cleaner place and move us closer to who and how we were born to live.

Soul Statement Example

My amends are cleansing me spiritually.

One big benefit of making amends is to be able to live unafraid of facing an uncomfortable part of you. Taking action to make appropriate amends should follow self-forgiveness. Self-forgiveness and amends together are critically important for getting clean and clear and increased inner peace becomes a natural byproduct.

Stop acting so small. You are the universe in ecstatic motion. ~ Rumi

Amends and Self-Forgiveness Practice

Make a list of past behaviors that you are not proud of. For each one, simply say to yourself, "*Yes, I did that.*" Make appropriate amends directly to the relevant person for each slight wherever possible and when to do so would not harm yourself or others. To gain the full power of this exercise, include self-forgiveness for each past behavior.

I found the following steps of Alcoholics Anonymous (AA) to be extremely helpful, irrespective of whether a person has an issue with alcohol. When done well, the doing of these steps is a demanding and spiritual journey of the highest order with great benefit.

Note: I recommend doing the AA Steps 8 through 10 with a trusted confidant, therapist or sponsor who has trod that ground before you. This person could be instrumental in helping you avoid common pitfalls and not inflict emotional injury to others.

AA Step Eight

(Alcoholics Anonymous: The Big Book; Fourth edition, 2002)
Made a list of all persons we had harmed, and became willing to make amends to them all.

AA Step Nine

(Alcoholics Anonymous: The Big Book; Fourth edition, 2002)
Made direct amends to such people wherever possible, except when to do so would injure them or others.

AA Step Ten

(Alcoholics Anonymous: The Big Book; Fourth edition, 2002)
We continued to take personal inventory and when we were wrong promptly admitted it.

Self-Assessment

Retreats, workshops and seminars are a type of community ritual. These shared activities are an excellent way to formally step back from life and reconnect with your deep self and what matters to you. However, not everyone can attend a formal multi-day event. Each of us, though, can make a list and honestly answer questions that one might be prompted to ask during a days-long soul-examination.

Self-Assessment Exercise

What feeds my spirit?
What am I afraid would happen if I said that out loud?
What have I been resisting?
Sometimes I pretend that...
What has my intuition been saying?
What small action could I take now to move in a better direction?

Truth-Telling

Issues simmer just below the surface when there isn't an acceptable and safe format to speak the unsaid. Inevitably, underlying (and undigested) feelings have a way of coming out sideways in the form of sarcastic or critical remarks or in jest or even anger. Sometimes, what is said jokingly may be actually be a test to gauge the reaction of others.

Staying current with interpersonal issues, rather than have them pile up into resentments, engenders safety, intimacy, trust and ease. I like the ritual of a truth-telling summit. This is when a couple or small group formally airs their true feelings and desires (hopefully with skillful communication and compassionate listening).

Unclogging stuck issues sooner than later can also help physical intimacy to occur in a more easy and natural fashion. Many couples that I know set aside regular times to sit knee-to-knee for the purpose of *clearing the air* between them. A trusted therapist and the use of Non-Violent Communication are appropriate resources for a truth-telling summit ritual. Truly high-functioning couples often have a weekly check-in to share what is working well and what could be improved. Forming clear and kind requests are an integral part of this being a useful and optimistic activity. It is key to have practices in place that consistently bring you into connection with your own heart and values. So that you are able to communicate appropriately and effectively. Don't just hope that you won't be an insensitive clod going forward. Tell yourself the truth, practice self-acceptance and put better strategies in place to support your honorable participation in your close relationships.

Personal Journaling Exercise
Do I usually speak from truth or let the moment pass?
Our current relationship truth-telling ritual is...
I wish our relationship truth-telling ritual would be...

Chapter Summary
Create a brief personal ritual (with a Soul Statement) that would consistently ground you into your core essence in the midst of daily life. Transform mundane transitions into holy moments.

Bring a little more of you to the room and to the moment. First go deep and then get going! Incorporate **Posture Points** as part of a greater mindfulness. Keep asking, "What feeds my spirit?" and choose to do that.

By using honest self-inquiry, you can learn to wield your energy with more conscious awareness. If you're not relishing something about yourself, release attachment to it. There is immense power in practicing forgiveness and making honest amends. Do what you must to arrive at self-forgiveness. Call upon courage (and an ally if needed) to make appropriate amends.

In the next chapter, we'll find more ways to discover what's alive and true on the inside and to trust love. Revolving on one's own axis and speaking op when feeling awkward will be addressed. It takes courage and a strong commitment to yourself in order to be willing to disappoint others in the service to your values.

We'll talk more about letting your feelings be trusted guides and many other tools and skills to support intimacy and clarity.

If you are moved to, tag me in a social media post describing how you have slowed down and become more mindful, with the hashtags #iamenough #slowingdown

8

INTERACTING WITH OTHERS

A person's success in life can usually be measured by the number of uncomfortable conversations he or she is willing to have.
~ Tim Ferriss

When we live from what's true, life gets easier. There is great benefit in showing up congruent with who you are at your depth. When you're aware of your deep values and core strength, it is natural to remain more balanced with your attention and speech. This way, you can be more responsive to what's happening in the present, rather than being distracted, or consumed, by an emotional over-hang. Staying in resonance with your deeper self, engenders self-assurance.

Soul Statement Example
I can contact the best of me.

Use a Soul Statement or other mini-ritual as needed prior to meeting up with another person to make a real-time connection with your heart. This will foster showing up for yourself in a more integrated way. With this practice, you may naturally experience more lightness and ease in interactions with other people.

Soul Statement Examples

I have strength and sureness at my core.
My distress is not a forever condition.

Stay On Your Own Axis

When you notice an energy drain (such as allowing a person to complain at length in your presence) you can restore balance by realizing the unhelpful nature of the event and stopping or exiting.

Saying, for example, *"I appreciate that this is a big deal for you and I have something pressing that I have to attend to."* You might also say something like, *"I appreciate there is a lot going on with you and I'm not able to hold that kind of space right now. Let's circle back at a better time."*

You may employ a silent Soul Statement to bring you back to center when you find yourself in a draining situation (such as, *"**I revolve around my own axis**"*). This sends a message to your brain that you are capable of dealing with anything, current situation included. It also serves as a reminder that your identity lives beyond circumstance.

A Soul Statement helps you see that the emotional flavor of the hour is fleeting. A Soul Statement helps put the moment in perspective and avoid being drawn into an upset. It will help diminish emotional triggering and foster emotional witness.

The state of emotional witness is where you can observe your thoughts and feelings without becoming embroiled in them. Achieving this makes it easier to notice a developing trigger and then address it before it overwhelms your system.

Attending to your emotional health is, metaphorically, putting the oxygen mask on yourself first. The more you take care of your emotional health, the more you can be present for others. An emotionally balanced person isn't dependent on any given interaction to fill something inside of them.

Soul Statement Examples
My inner peace is always accessible.
My happiness is best sourced from within.

Your chosen beloved should not be viewed as the source of your happiness, love or pleasure. This person is simply whom you get to express love with. Of foundational importance to healthy intimate relating is to be responsible for your own happiness. Looking for happiness or other fulfillment externally is a never-ending quest. Perhaps the world is designed to disappoint so that we will eventually look inward for answers.

Consider adopting an attitude of, *"What do I have to offer this person?"*, versus *"What will I get from our time together?"* As part of a *checkup from the heart up* prior to meeting an intimate partner, ask yourself, *"Am I clinging or am I bringing?"* In other words, are you anticipating that something from they will fill you or are you intending to participate in co-creating a beautiful experience together?

I want to show up for my intimate partner (and all of life) resourced and rested. We both are well-served when I get clear and right with myself while alone and then arrive in a secure state and truly ready to be together. It's imperative that I show up with a *full tank of gas* emotionally, more often than I show up depleted, deflated or over-tired.

Soul Statement Example
My self-care nourishes me.

A depleted, *empty well* version of you that keeps trudging from task to task is not the best way to serve life, even in the short term. Just as you learned to pay attention to your bodily needs, you can learn to pay attention to your emotional fill levels. Asking the simple question, *"How full is my tank?"* will go a long way toward awareness of when adjustments are needed.

Ask Practice (prior to meeting a beloved)
How full is my tank and what would help me at this time?
Have I communicated what would help me?
Am I clinging or am I bringing?

Meeting Your Partner
A meetup can either be just another part of a busy day, or an opportunity for intentional connection. Are you happy with the current pattern of relating with your partner? Do you or they offer praise or touch? Do you take a moment for stillness together? Do you allow each other *space to land* before sharing information?

Enriching conversation is not just information exchange. Your partner is usually not better off when you attempt to re-connect by first sharing a surface story or point of interest. Your intimate partner does not need a news update as much as they need to feel that you're with them in real time and that they matter.

Personal Journaling Exercise
Am I as connected to my core values as I can be?

Being interested in what is going on for them and, when appropriate, offering a sense of what is going on in you fosters trust and ease. It feels good to be in curiosity about what is up for another person. "*How are you feeling about that?*" is often a good response to another person's news report.

You don't have to make it a big deal every time you greet each other. The event can simply be made more special by offering warmth. If you want to create a different pattern with regards to how you meet after an absence, find a neutral time with your partner and discuss what already works and what you would like to add, remove or modify.

Soul Statement Example

I am not my story.

Avoid assigning meaning to another person's actions. Deciding what someone else's motivations were for a given action is a recipe for conflict. This can feel demeaning or belittling when it is done to you.

When you are subjected to someone else deciding your feelings or motivation, instead of saying, "*Don't tell me what I'm feeling!*" a more skillful response, after a silent Soul Statement such as, "**My heart is secure.**", might be, "*I'm not going to take on your assessment. Are you open to hearing my motivation for that action?*".

Trust Love

I'd been camping in the Back of Beyond for five weeks. Every day I hiked by myself for up to nine hours in order to find safe travel routes and water sources for an expedition that I was supervising in the convoluted canyon and mesa country.

One day I discovered an old, abandoned track that went through thick timber on the northerly side of a ridge. What a pleasure it was to walk on level ground without obstacles! I kept my eyes down as I let myself become lost in deep thought.

I walked by numerous many anthills had been dug into and wondered why. (Hint: Bears love to dig anthills so they can lick the ants off their paws.) Coming around a bend it occurred me to look up, and there was a mama bear and her cub right there in the middle of the trail. She was standing on her hind legs with the cub at her feet just 10 yards in front of me.

This was a moment of truth. I could feel the bear's surprise. I sensed that she was withholding judgment as she watched for my next move. The cub stared at me while pressed tightly to mama bear's legs. Dappled sunlight shone on their cinnamon-colored fur. I was struck by the beauty and power compressed into this moment.

If I ran, the bear would be on me before I had taken three steps. If I bluffed in anger, she would accept the challenge and fight to protect her cub. I felt that my only route to a happy outcome was to remain still and inhabit love. I felt my heart open and I let love and admiration energetically flow over to her. I let myself be transfixed in beauty. I stopped thinking and just felt wonder and caring for these magnificent creatures.

After a minute, I slowly turned my palms outward and softly spoke, "I love you." At hearing this, mama bear dropped to all fours while the cub scampered up the hill. Mama bear glanced in the direction of the cub, looked back at me and then walked up into the trees after her little one. I moved slowly and quietly back around the bend and sat on a log. I gave them a half hour of space before proceeding on my way.

Years later I was the field director of a wilderness-based drug recovery program. In one instance, there was a recent arrival who was just a few days removed from regular methamphetamine use. This young man decided that our group was not the place for him and he was determined to strike out for civilization on his own.

In order to help him stay safe, one of the instructors and I walked with him. As we walked, I spent time talking with this aggrieved man for a while. As he was fixed in his purpose, I re-joined the instructor while we followed behind at a distance. As the afternoon turned to night, this young person became increasingly belligerent, and so we lagged farther behind to give him more breathing room.

The young man began yelling insults at us and threatening us with harm, yet we did not engage. The instructor and I walked without speaking as the young man continued to rant. This went on for a while and by now it was full dark. He had stopped yelling and so we picked up the pace in order to monitor his whereabouts. When we came around a bend in the trail the young man was right in front of us. He had stopped and was waiting for us to catch up.

We stood where we were to see what he would do. The young man walked toward me and I immediately thought, "He might do me harm." I did not know his intentions, but I decided to suspend judgement and trust that I could handle whatever he intended to do.

He stepped in close, raised his arms and gave me a hug. It was real. He had calmed down, thought things over and decided that we were his allies. We all returned to camp and he finished the six-week program in good form.

Just like with the bear encounter, if I had responded to the unstable and unpredictable man in the dark in an aggressive or defensive way any trust or goodwill would have evaporated and that man's life would have taken a worse turn. If I had done anything but stand still and feel wonder for the beauty in front of me, that mama bear might very well have hurt me badly. In both instances, my decision to trust love made all the difference.

Soul Statement Examples

There is love inside me.

When I trust love, I can handle what happens.

Feelings Before Information

Ubiquitous *tech-no-logic* devices act to separate us from what we may be feeling in the moment. Most of us, most of the time, respond to the question, "*What's happening?*", by referencing a current state of doing rather than a feeling.

If someone asks, "*What are you feeling?*", you may often not know how to answer right then. If the question is, "*What are you thinking?*", then, I suspect, you would have an easy, quick answer.

Information will keep you in your head. Do feelings before information. Be curious about what is interesting and important to others. One of my friends is a great role model in that she will catch herself 'reporting' in mid-sentence, pause and start over with something like, "*Oh, hello friend. I am glad you're here and I'm happy to see you.*"

Soul Statement Examples

I am a human being. I can just be.
My deep self is my security.

An intimate partner cannot be your essential muse if you're unaware of their inner winds. You don't really learn about a person unless you are aware of what moves, contracts and expands them. Expressing true interest will help you gain a window into their world.

I regularly ask my partner for an "*emotional weather report*". This may sound like, "*What is happening with you on the inside?*". When I say, "*What's the weather?*", she knows that I'm referring to her internal weather. Earnest questions will take you a long way into connection.

Emotional Weather Report Practice

Ask for an emotional weather report. Respect what is said in reply.

Small talk is its own special enjoyment and it's okay to go beyond it at times. You can confess dislike of small talk that seems to circle into nowhere. Firstly, look at how much you feed in to small talk, or even gossip. Secondly, be secure enough in who you are so that you don't need to share the latest triumph or pain in every conversation. Consider making your *complaint fast* into a *complaint & gossip fast*.

With a secure internal foundation, made more accessible with regular Soul Statements, you can just be interested in connection that is occurring in real time. Ideally your inner experience is handled appropriately in other settings, so there isn't the need to go over-deep in an otherwise light exchange.

When meeting a new person, I will sometimes say, *"I want to get to know you better. What do you like other people to know about you?"* Just ask a question and listen deeply to their answer. Being authentically interested in a person builds connection more readily than attempting to be clever or interesting, which Stephen R. Covey describes in his book, *The 7 Habits of Highly Effective People*.

The most important question is the follow up question. Inquiring about answers shows that you are actually paying attention versus just making conversation. You might respond with, *"What does that mean to you?"* Think, less information reporting and more curiosity. We offer dignity to a person when we acknowledge them as bigger than their surface story. You might then be rewarded with a larger window into their world.

Remember that each person has struggled in some way and assume that they have something to teach you. This is one way to develop more empathy as a habitual attitude. The wise teacher, Baba Dez Nichols, says, *"If you can't see God in this person, proceed no further."*

Connecting Questions

I admire X quality in you. Where does that come from?
Since I don't know you well, would you mind sharing what's important to you?
Why is that important to you?
What do you like other people to know about you?

External Cues

There are external cues of when it's a good time to tune up. These cues relate to how the world responds to you. If you've disturbed your intimate partner, he/she/they may present as anxious or critical. Perhaps you went on too long with a story versus simply articulating what is important?

Typically, other people are less enthusiastic about being in your presence when you talk at length. A good clue may be when the person you're with stops asking questions. To counteract this tendency, consider the practice of talking for a maximum of two minutes before asking your companion about THEIR thoughts.

Personal Journaling Exercise

Some of my external cues of when to tune up are...

A friend once gave an elegant example of the importance of tuning up. My girlfriend was in a bit of distress and apologized to him for being sensitive. My friend said, "*On the contrary, your attunement is a valuable flag for me to tune up my own sensitivity.*" Think of your partner as an *emotional weathervane* who is more sensitive than you. While listening to them speak, give your mind a rest. If you listen in an undefended manner, you can better hear what is critical to know about how other people experience you.

Soul Statement Examples
I am well-served by tuning up.
I can trust my inner compass.

Courage to Be Clear

I employ the term **Courage to Be Clear** to describe the practice of speaking up when something feels uncomfortable or *off*. When your **Courage to Be Clear** commitment is functioning, you can more easily address a given issue while it is still emerging.

You may be a activating a new and unfamiliar social muscle to speak up when something feels minor rather than waiting until it becomes super-uncomfortable. Yes, it takes courage to address a smaller issue rather than wait for it to be so big that there is no way to step around it.

As we all know, big stuff often starts out as small stuff. Why not bring something up while it still has a relatively low charge attached? In practice, this can simply be asking about what is occurring. Think of this as *doing the emotional dishes* versus letting feelings or problems pile up.

Employing the **Courage to Be Clear** in real time requires a commitment to fearlessness. This type of fearlessness can translate into a willingness to initiate a potentially difficult or awkward conversation. I've found that is usually better to discuss a still-emerging issue before any emotional charge gains unhelpful velocity. Consider feeling a bit uncomfortable as a call to appreciate your own sensitivity and respond by aligning your next action with how you wish to show up for yourself and others.

It's one thing to notice an emerging issue and another level of bravery to honor and speak to it in the moment. Personally, I want to know when there is a ripple or contraction in the shared field. Perhaps I have inadvertently created a misunderstanding. It feels good to act in congruence with one's own self-image and address strangeness or discomfort sooner than later. A good real-time prompt is to ask yourself is, *"How would the best version of me respond right now?"*

Avoiding difficult subjects does not lead to an easy life. Being willing to have difficult conversations leads to greater freedom, integrity and choice. I love being around friends whose **Courage to Be Clear** is highly developed. If they sense a strangeness in the shared field or an incongruent voice tone, they will simply ask for more information without adding a charge to it.

Soul Statement Example
I'm empowered by clarity.

Clarity helps friends stay friends. I would rather hear about something small in close to real time while perhaps I can still do something about it as opposed to hearing afterward when there's a history that I cannot change. Acting with fearlessness doesn't mean waiting until all fear is dissipated. It just means to *fear less* and take the next best action, however small.

> *Courage is what it takes to stand up and speak; courage is also what it takes to sit down and listen.* ~ Winston Churchill

When you feel an energy shift, the fearless version of you can speak up and ask what is going on. This may sound like, *"I would like to press pause and speak to what I just felt"* or, *"I hear your words and I'm also feeling something else. Can we speak directly to that?"*.

Courage to Be Clear as a practice, permits others to meet you with enhanced authenticity. It is not your responsibility to caretake or calm another person's emotions, but speaking up in the interest of clear communication generally serves all parties. When two persons have clear communication and open hearts – that's a win. Being transparent and kind is a win.

An emerging issue can be an opportunity to feel your value and your values. You may think of your *Courage to Be Clear* as a valuable early-warning response to help keep conversations upfront and respectful.

When you draw upon the *Courage to Be Clear* to identify what's alive in you, you're better able to speak from a more certain and informed place (ideally with a measure of grace and skill). Remember to flex your honesty muscles with kindness.

Soul Statement Example

Being clear and transparent supports my interactions.

Nice is Over-Rated

People tend to feel more secure with the person who is upfront with what they're about and who makes clear what they want. People don't necessarily feel safer around a person with no needs. In a sense, my 'nice guy' persona was a mask (or guise) that I hid behind for most of my life. This allowed me to remain living as a smaller version of me. The physical and emotional safety that I thought this would give was yet another delusion.

In his book, *Don't Be Nice, Be Real,* author Kelly Bryson employs the term, *nice guise.* The nice guise that I wore certainly did not serve anyone, including me. In order to drop a nice guise persona, it isn't necessary to practice a new you. You only need to stop doing all the stuff that isn't in congruence with your true nature.

Feel yourself in a deep way, so that your partner can then feel you. You're best-served to be rested and resourced before coming together with a beloved. The setup is before you meet. Check the nice persona at the door. Don't be the safe person who hides their passion behind a nice mask. Be the transparent person, even if it is not so neat and orderly.

Soul Statement Example
My open heart is precious.

When appropriate, communicate what is happening to your partner in a respectful manner. This may sound like, *"I need to express some thoughts / feelings"* or, *"I'm requesting a short separation."* When alone you may roar like a jungle cat or scream with your hand cupped over your mouth or make your own entertainment or artistry. You could also journal and invent new phrases or words to reflect your inner process.

Personal Journaling Exercise
Do I always speak directly and honestly to my needs?
Do I feel sidelined or "not listened to" when I state
what I really need?
What am I afraid might happen if I speak directly to my needs?
When could I speak up for my needs going forward?

Be Brave Enough to Disappoint
The more I slow down to remain centered, the better I am able to be present for anyone else. Self-connection should come before any other connections. I want my beloved to feel that she is glad to have chosen to spend her time with me. This being said, I have to sometimes be willing to disappoint her in the short term in order to take care of me (and by extension our quality of interaction).

Soul Statement Example

My self-connection is paramount.

Your intimate partner shouldn't be meant to feel like just another thing on a To-Do list. Ideally, your partner feels you acknowledging their heart in real time. I've found that the best connection outcomes often occur when a person offers undefended openness. You can facilitate this by a self-checkup before coming to your partner. **Tip**: There doesn't need to be distress in order to show affection.

If you find yourself backsliding into complaining or other old pattern, skip an excuse and just re-anchor to the truth of who and what you are. A self-checkup can simply be a pause to feel your own depth of presence.

Self-Checkup Questions

Am I aware of my body?
Am I conscious of my own needs?
Am I able to be present and listen?
Am I capable of offering love and humor and light?

Keep Going

One time I was bucked off a horse while riding alone in the redwood forest. I couldn't move for the shock and pain of broken bones and a collapsed lung. I also couldn't stay where I was. I had not informed anyone at the ranch that I had gone riding.

While I was lying on the ground, I recalled a time years before, on a Search and Rescue mission, when I followed the arduous track of a woman who'd gotten lost in the dark and fallen off a New Mexico cliff. Despite multiple broken bones, she mustered the grit to agonizingly crawl toward the light of a far-off house during a bitter cold night. She finally made it to this house that next morning. As known trackers, my best friend and I had been called to find her still-missing dog, whom we miraculously located and rescued.

I now faced the same decision as this woman had. I could stay put and likely go into shock, or slowly and painfully move toward help. So, I began to slowly inch my way toward home. Fortunately, I was discovered by a party of friends who had ventured out to find me in the night.

Sometimes we have to be willing to feel the pain of emotional wounding and keep going. In the aftermath of one particularly painful relationship breakup, I decided that I wouldn't let pain close my heart. My choice going forward into an unknown future was to love no matter what.

Soul Statement Examples

I can love no matter what (because love is who I am).
There is grit inside me that I can call upon.

Chapter Summary

Use Soul Statements to make a real-time connection with your heart. When we live from what's true, life gets easier.

Let being informed from your heart elevate your conversations. Show up for your intimate partner (and all of life) resourced and rested. Be honest when deciding if you are *bringing or clinging*. Don't just practice appreciation, make appreciation a practice.

Do feelings BEFORE information. Be curious about what is interesting and important to others. Earnest questions will take you a long way into connection, discovery and intimacy.

Ask for an emotional weather report and listen to the answer. Cultivate your **Courage to Be Clear**. Keep up with doing the *emotional dishes*.

In the next chapter you'll discover the importance of acknowledgement as well as simple tools to increase openheartedness. You'll see how the over-polite person is boring.

We'll discuss the power of invitations and requests and of the **Re-do**. Speaking the unsaid will also be a theme. We don't have all the answers, but we are gaining tools and resources.

If you are moved to, tag me in a social media post about how to stay on your own axis and trust love, with the hashtags #getbetter #trustlove

9

INTIMATE RELATIONSHIP COMMUNICATION

Life shrinks or expands in proportion to one's courage. ~ Anaïs Nin

We've all had some amount of pain that comes from living out poor patterns in intimate relationship. (For example: no safe way to address difficult subjects, not speaking directly to your needs or giving attention to the children whilst saving little to no energy for your partner.) For better communication, talk less and listen more. If you distill an issue into its essence you'll be more easily understood and less boring.

Soul Statement Example
Love is who and what and why I am.

Long explanations dilute the power of an apology or position. My coaching clients consistently find that using less words is cleaner and more effective, which leads to quicker resolution. This will help you communicate your desires in simple, clear terms.

Staying clear and up-to-date with interpersonal issues supports intimacy. Are there unacknowledged or unspoken rules that place touchy subjects off-limits in your intimate relationships? Is truth valued by both of you? Is taking swift ownership for one's actions standard? Do either of you go silent versus speak directly to a problem? Does one person typically storm off rather than stay and solve a disturbance? The good news is that skillful communication can be developed and improved upon.

Soul Statement Example
Serenity and ease are available to me.

To make difficult conversations less difficult, make truth and transparency part of normal conversation. Keep the focus on feelings, impact and needs going forward versus what the other person did or didn't do. How you communicate with a beloved is more important than the specific words you choose.

A worthy goal is loving acceptance of each other's reality and reactions. Saying things in a positive way can be a stand-alone spiritual practice. Have values-centered conversations more often than complaint-centered conversations. Soul Statements will help keep the focus on what you value.

Personal Journaling Exercise
Our intimate relationship structure for information,
requests and truth-telling is...
What I wish this structure to be is...

Your partner's internal experience of your togetherness is need-to-know information. A shouting contest of who has been most wronged is counterproductive at best. Begin with a willingness to accept the impact of your words and actions versus arguing for the validity of your own experience. Choose to slow down into presence and curiosity. As Jocko Willink says, *"The more I listen, the more I see"*.

Soul Statement Examples
My Inner Guidance is available.
My Inner Guidance is spot-on.

When you feel more resourced (having a full *emotional pantry*, if you will) you can better navigate rough patches. Among these resources is perspective. It's often helpful to remember that this person you've chosen to be with is perfectly human. Consider that their responses are completely normal given their unique history and pressures.

It is useful to think of your partner as an important teacher who has been molded and prepared by life to bring forth precisely what you are most needing in order to grow as a person.

My woman is a finely-tuned emotional bio-feedback device that's calibrated to notice my drift (away from my centerline of grounded clarity) in real-time. She will notice, before I do, when my attention wanes or wanders. This being the case, I have many tools to make my own adjustments and I'm committed to my own growth.

You are flying blind if you don't know what's in your partner's heart. When you identify a need of another person it allows you to more easily reach a place of empathy. Consider their needs as arising from a beautiful place. I want to benefit from my beloved's perspective and the way she brings light to each moment. I want to know what affects her and how deeply she perceives. Owning one's own needs and choosing empathy is an evolved way of living.

Each feeling that you hold back, whether based in fear or joy, can be thought of as an emotional brick. With enough bricks in place, a wall forms. Each time you offer vulnerable honesty you're essentially removing an emotional brick. Luckily, good communication doesn't require an advanced rocket science degree. It does require an open mind and heart and a commitment to acting better. Whether you're currently in an intimate relationship or not you can view feedback from others as a chance to improve your communication skills.

Soul Statement Example
My self-care is an act of love.

First Listen and Acknowledge. Then, Give.
To get to the other side of a distress event it is generally most effective to first salve, then solve. **Listen** and **Acknowledge** first (salve). Then **Give** second (solve). If you jump right into solutions, you risk having the other person feel that acknowledging their pain was skipped and was therefore discounted.

A good and workable and lasting solution will typically be discovered AFTER acknowledging feelings and uncovering needs. Make it your practice to discover your companion's needs before sharing your own and watch your interactions change for the better.

Resist the habit of *giving in* in order to find a place where you may each *give to*. Don't offer solutions until the other person is ready to hear your ideas. Restore alignment (and connection) in an intimate relationship by acknowledging the other person for what they just said. Don't rush past this moment. Learn to hold space and respectfully listen without needing to share your point of view. Feel whatever has come up together and let it steep. Letting it steep will increase compassion for each other and respect for each other's experience. Acknowledge, Acknowledge, Acknowledge. Do not skip acknowledgment. Ever.

Ask Yourself

Have I heard what the person in front of me is saying?

Does this person feel acknowledged?

Is there a clear request?

Have I asked what they need?

How You Argue

It matters how you argue. Without a respectful and effective mechanism for resolving conflict you shouldn't engage in conflict. It's simply too damaging. Don't try to teach your partner anything when they or you are in a triggered state.

How do you feel when your partner attempts to teach you how to behave in the middle of an upset? Why would someone want to listen to you when you've ignored what they just said? Learn to share your truth in a way that doesn't negate your partner's truth. Connect inside to what you are willing to offer.

If a less-than-happy event from the past gets brought forth, none of us can go back in time and deal with it differently. Simply acknowledge any behavioral slip and ask what your companion is needing. See if you can feel the valid need under the other person's stated desires. Be curious about what is alive in them. Listen closely for their value that was not being met. Some examples of relevant values are: safety, dignity, respect, consideration, autonomy and support.

One way to avoid laying an *emotional minefield* for your partner is to find a neutral time to share what gets you most upset. When you have a respectful system to address issues (ideally in close to real time), hurt feelings don't have a chance to grow bigger than need be.

It is all too easy to end up arguing about a poorly executed process versus a desired outcome. It's okay to talk about bothersome behaviors, but not okay to attack and accuse one another. If one person is doing 90% of the talking, then that is not a healthy discussion.

When a misstep occurs, the real test is whether or not you can recover and access your truer, deeper self and act better in real-time. You cannot talk your way into truth with an intimate partner. The best you can do is to be present as fully as you know how.

You may have to adjust your physical posture and change your voice tone to access the best version of yourself. Employ a silent Soul Statement such as, "**I am true and can act true.**" Do what it takes to act with greater congruency. Explore ways to keep your emotional well full so that you're better resourced when moments of test or trial appear.

Aspire to speak directly to what's true. Say, "*I'd rather not be doing this right now*", if that is real. You might remind your partner that you are practicing an authentic, "*No*", and that you welcome the same from they. Do not toy with your partner's psyche, just be real with kindness. Give your love, humor, presence, confidence and patience no matter what tests may come. Test will always come. Your response to a test is what cements or dissolves that particular date with your power.

Over-Politeness

Over-politeness equals death in intimate relationship. **If you want to get better, you must face difficult emotions and embrace awkward conversations**. Practice un-metering your passion in private. We are all works in progress and no one is watching. Think of your private expression as a mediocre first draft of a more empowered you.

Being overly polite is a version of playing small. For much of my life, I turned down my enthusiasm when an intimate partner was stressed or tired. I had a tendency to follow the other person's moods or energy rather than offer stable, centered strength.

Overcoming the habit of being a *pleaser* or my *too nice* conditioning sometimes felt as if I was trying to turn around an aircraft carrier. Other times I would step up and claim my voice and power in the moment. Not holding myself back with consistency was a multi-year challenge, but well worth doing.

A girlfriend once gave me a wakeup call when I gave her a brief kiss. She looked me square in the eyes and exclaimed, *"Don't just half-kiss me!"*. Wow! I got it right then that the kiss was indicative of how I was not owning my desire and my *Grrr*. I got it and stepped up my game. Act more in alignment with your best self by making a positive shift the moment that you notice you're slipping into an incongruent behavior.

Non-Violent Communication (NVC) teaches that anger occurs when we are not in touch with our needs. Frame your thinking and intimate conversations in terms of met or unmet needs. Do not teach your partner how to behave, just stay with communicating your own feelings.

Too often when a person leads off an exchange by advocating for their own pain and tries to articulate how they were wronged (in graphic detail), it has the effect of inflicting pain on the listener. When you lead with feelings, it is more likely that you may be able to discover and validate an unmet need together. Ask, *"How can I skillfully make my needs known?"*.

Real-Time Questions

Am I offering love to my own tense or fearful heart?

What can I do right now to best serve love?

How quickly can we return to love?

When another person is speaking of their upset, you might help them identify and communicate their unmet and important need by saying, *"I hear what you're saying, but I'm not clear what you are needing?*

Or simply, *"I get that you are upset. What would help you in this moment?"* Listen closely to the reply. Acknowledge what is said before proceeding.

Soul Statement Example
Openheartedness is my natural state.

Do not require perfection from your partner or yourself. Allow each other to be messy while adopting new language and behavior. When you stumble, just create another flow chart of behavior. Up-level your presence. Acknowledge and address unmet needs.

Celebrate when needs are met. Recognize and make small bids for connection. Over-reward the smallest try (weighted to behavior, not words). The benefits of these practices may be small at first, but remember, direction is more important than speed.

Intent Matters Less Than Impact
It is important to bust the fantasy of how you imagine that you come off as opposed to how you actually behave. Listen to your partner to hear what is important to know about your own behavior. **You are the expert on your intention and everyone else is an expert on your impact.** Be willing to do what is difficult poorly at first in order to build your undefended intimacy muscles.

People often argue at length in an effort to explain and defend their intention. One's intention actually matters very little as compared to one's impact on others. Your intent is of negligible value when another person feels harmed by you. It is a better use of your time to seek to understand the impact of your actions. Be open to hearing what hurts your companion. Be willing to speak truth to yourself on the inside.

Soul Statement Examples
I benefit from knowing my impact on others.
My slip-ups are opportunities to grow.

I understand the impact of my actions better when my partner speaks directly to her present-time feeling. It is communication gold to hear exactly how a beloved wishes to be received or responded to in a given situation. It is generally helpful to make a conversation less about story and more about feelings and what would help each of you now. Use the formula, **"I feel X and I need Y"** as a guide. Assigning of motives to another person is an evaluation and generally counterproductive.

When you are the one feeling distress, speak succinctly about your experience by leading with the impact on you versus a critique of the other person or instruction regarding how you want them to act. Simply state, **"I'm feeling X."** Behaving badly, due to a current upset, is the enemy, not your partner. Keep returning to what you're feeling versus attempting to argue a story.

Too often we want our ego salved by letting another person know that they were wrong. People are typically more receptive to hearing your upset if the communication begins with the impact of said actions rather than with some form of, *"You did this and I don't like it."*

Speaking from your own experience is a foundational interpersonal communication skill. *"YOU did X and YOU are a dummy-dog, so YOU caused me to feel like crap!"*, is not a great formula to initiate a connecting dialog. It is especially potent to lead with a feeling word. This can be as simple as, **"I feel X."** To incorporate a request, you might say, **"I feel X and I need Y."** Further explanation often diminishes the potency of your communication and provides content that may be argued with.

It is wise to avoid telling another person your assessment of their action and instead share how their action impacted you. Give yourself a silent Soul Statement reminder like, "*Their evaluation does not describe me.*" Then briefly share how you've been affected and conclude with a clear request. You will likely find that other people are more at ease and natural around you when you do this consistently.

Leading with Impact and Needs Examples

I'm not feeling great right now. Let's figure out something different.
I feel contracted and I need tenderness.
A loss of trust happened and what would help me now is gentleness and openness.
I feel concerned when you weren't here at the agreed time. In the future, I would like a timely message if you're running late.

Invitations and Requests

What if the Universal Field that surrounds and imbues all matter responds to the energy of an invitation? What if free will and the ability to choose means that you're on your own until you make a formal request of your guardian angels?

I'm a fan of reminding the universe (and my own psyche) of who I am and what I need. Why wouldn't you want to provide clarity to your angel team? They may be waiting for permission to step in and give assistance.

You can support congruency and greater ease in your life by making verbal requests. In any case, life can become simple by matching invitations to desires. When you're lonely, call someone. When you want to be alone, make it happen. When feeling appreciation or love or respect, speak it out loud. Say what you are up for and not up for. Invite others to do the same.

Remember, it's okay to be messy with language as you practice making your desires known. Clear requests are how you convert an unsaid complaint into a verbal ask. Sincere requests can lead you further into connection. Practice making consistent verbal requests that are simple, direct, kind and clear and notice how your life changes. **Note**: If a person consistently responds poorly to this type of gracious clarity, you may have to lessen or modify your interaction with them.

Identify and ask for your heart's desire. Your heart's desire, in this case, refers to whatever the most fulfilling experience would be if you could have your way. This is sometimes difficult, but how else will others know what serves you best?

Make a request when something is not in line with your heart's desire. An example of speaking this way is, *"My heart's desire is to spend an hour by myself before we run out to the market."* Another example, *"Your offer is appealing and my heart's desire is to attend the Jade Festival that weekend."* Clear requests that language a valid need go a long way toward heartfelt connection.

Soul Statement Examples
My heart's desire is important and worthy of regard.
Making clear invitations supports my ease.

Your ability to engage can be communicated as, *"My tank is 70 percent full"* or *"On a scale of 1 to 10, I can only show up at a 6 right now."* You might say, *"You are important to me and I can be more present for you after I take a shower and get something to eat."* A *"No for now"* makes a *"Yes"* sweeter and more trustable when it happens.

Making clear invitations and speaking your heart's desire will lead you on a path to greater ease. Employing a silent Soul Statement can also help you clarify your message to speak your needs in a simple, direct and caring manner.

Personal Journaling Exercise
What invitations have I made in the last week and month?
What invitations have I passed on making in the last week
and month?
What invitations will I make going forward?

Turn complaints into clear requests. For example, *"What would help me right now is…"* and *"Are you open to hearing how I want this communicated to me?"* You can also help someone formulate a request by asking, *"What do you need right now?"*. Stay plugged in to your power so you may *speak from deep* with clear requests. Ask simple, direct questions as needed to increase clarity.

Soul Statement Examples
My center informs my requests.
I am bigger than any complaint.

The Re-do
I'm a big fan of the **Re-do**. The **Re-do** is simply noticing that you have been speaking or acting poorly, and doing it over in a better fashion. Apply a relevant Soul Statement to re-align your focus in order to feel ready to offer the best of you. Use the power of the **Re-do** to shift from a less-than-optimal exchange into one that better reflects how you wish to act.

Re-do Communication Examples
I'm sorry for how that sounded. How I really want to say it is…
This old behavior isn't working for me anymore. I want to
Re-do it in a better way.

What you say is important and when you speak in that tone,
I have trouble hearing you.
I know you love me, but that didn't sound loving. Would you
please start over?
Are you open to hearing how I would prefer to be spoken to?

As you become more practiced, formality can be dropped and sometimes a code word will suffice. One person may just say, *"Re-do"* (perhaps with a raised eyebrow). Boom! Game on. Time to get right on the inside. Act better and back yourself out of the relational boggy ground.

Soul Statement Example
In order to step up, I remember who and what I am.

Speak the Unsaid
Clarity and safety come from respectfully talking about sensitive issues. With my coaching clients, I often encourage the unsaid to become the said in an appropriate and respectful form. What's held in eventually comes out sideways in less-than-useful or hurtful ways. A check-in to appropriately and respectfully speak what has been held back is a good place to begin an inquiry about each other's experience.

When is the last time that you and your partner spoke directly about what is working and what isn't with regards to your relationship? Were either of you open or were you defensive and did that change during the conversation? How large is the gap between your ideal relating and the current situation?

The only thing harder than being a saint, is living with one.

When you learn to speak the unsaid with grace there will typically be less that is left unsaid. Create a togetherness that can handle truth-telling. Building honesty muscles is similar to working out in the gym. A life of honesty takes doing hard things with consistency and commitment. Don't allow an issue to build up such that it becomes too big to tackle. If things are going to get better, you have to speak the unspoken.

Soul Statement Examples
Undefended truth is an aphrodisiac.
I am capable of strengthening my honesty muscle.

Reid Mihalko's Difficult Conversation Formula
(Reid is a communication ninja.) Adapted and used with permission. Original version is at www.ReidAboutSex.com

Step 1: Take time alone and write the answers to the following questions:

1. What I'm not saying is...

2. What I'm afraid might happen if I say this out loud is...

3. What I'd like to have happen by saying this is...

Step 2: Insert your answers into the script below, which you can memorize or read from.
(It can also be the script that you send via email, etc.)

Step 3: Share your issue by following the script below. (Ideally, find a time when the other person has some neutrality and bandwidth to listen.)

Optional lead-in: *"I want to share something in the interest of increasing our trust and connection. (And, you haven't done anything wrong.) Is this a good time for that?"*

Script: *"There is something I've not been saying to you. I haven't yet been able to say it, because I'm afraid the following might happen..."* (**Answers from B here**)

"What I would like to have happen by sharing with you is..." (**Answers from C here**)

"What I haven't been telling you is..." (**Answer from A here**).

"Thank you for listening. What, if anything, would you like to say?"

Give Good Phone

The importance of speaking directly to feelings is critical over the phone since body language is absent. Even on Zoom or FaceTime, something is lost via the screen. It is often very helpful to mention how the sound of their voice affects you or that you're thinking of how beautiful they must be at this moment.

Challenge yourself to give more love, presence and attention during phone interactions with your intimate partner. Extra points get awarded for offering acknowledgment and understanding!

A silent Soul Statement with a conscious breath just before

picking up can help transition your attention. Doesn't your beloved deserve good phone? If something else requires steady focus it's often better to let the call go to voicemail.

Whether talking about mundane topics or intimate subjects (like desire or dreams) you'll do better when it's clear to each person which purpose a given phone call is serving.

It's also helpful to have formal transitions from one type of topic to another. Say, for instance, *"I'm enjoying our talk AND I need to change the subject. Do you need anything else before we shift gears?"*

The more you can own what you like, the more erotic a phone call can be. The more detailed the fantasy, the more interesting it will be to both of you. Think, *'**aural sex**'*. *"Oh yeah baby, I'll come home and you'll do me"*, is much less captivating than, *"When I walk through the door, I want you wearing a short skirt and no panties. You'll be in the laundry room pretending that you haven't heard me enter the house. I'll see the light on and find you there. I'll say your name in a deep voice and..."* You get the idea!

Soul Statement Example
I can bring forth the best of me.

Return to Love with a Repair Conversation
Sometimes a repair conversation is in order when balance and harmony have been damaged. To have a repair conversation, begin by being connected to your center and deeply listen to what matters to your companion. Don't try to engage with the skillset and mindset that has led to grief.

Openhearted connection must come BEFORE strategy for resolving a point of contention. A solution often becomes more obvious once you're in a place of compassion and understanding for each other's needs, fears and desires. When you acknowledge and accept the other person's pain your own heart will often feel spontaneous generosity. You can explore a strategy for resolving an issue AFTER you've reached a place of understanding and openheartedness.

Intimacy builds the bonds of love. Intimacy is nourished by connection and trust. Connection is an essential relationship ingredient that must be actively nurtured. Create moments of connection and be worthy of trust. Keep adding weight to the right side of the connection scale. Keep making deposits into the *emotional bank account*. Acting badly is making a withdrawal from the *emotional bank account*.

Real-Time Questions

What is a good Soul Statement for me right now?

What can I do to help us return to love?

Am I able to be present enough to listen well?

Can I over-respond in a good way right now to this ripple/disturbance in the field?

How might I phrase a clear request?

Chapter Summary

Talk less and listen more. Learn to accept the impact you've had versus arguing for the validity of your own experience.

Listen and acknowledge, then give as an evolved way of living. Do not require perfection from your partner or yourself. Allow each other to be messy while adopting new behavior.

Lead with feelings and needs over a version of events. Use, *"I feel X and I need Y."* Trade complaints for invitations and clear requests (and watch your world change). Enact a **Re-do** as appropriate. Move into finding a mutually beneficial strategy AFTER you've found a place of understanding and openheartedness. Speak the unsaid (and remember to give good phone).

In the next chapter, we'll address the emotionally triggered state, which I term, **The Mist**. I'll also present an expanded list of "**F**" word responses and how to self-soothe in times of distress.

If you are moved to, tag me in a social media post about how speaking the unsaid has benefited you with the hashtag #speaktruth #iamfree

INTIMATE RELATIONSHIP DISTRESS

*Self-connectedness must be the center
and love the circumference. ~ Osho*

After decades of relationship heartache and tribulation I discovered that most relationships don't end for lack of love, but for lack of intimacy. Whether sexual or emotional, intimacy fosters bonding and optimism. The longer a couple goes without intimacy, the harder it seems to return to it.

Soul Statement Example
*I've walked through hotter fire than this
and I am clear on the inside.*

There is a cultural expectation to be a great lover and communicator in intimate relationship, but where is the training for this? Our family of origin, friends, TV sitcoms, movies and social media platforms provide much of the interpersonal modeling today. Intimacy tools are mostly gotten through osmosis in our culture.

This means that your parents are, to some extent, your relationship gurus. They are not always the best models for creating deep, lasting intimacy or for skillfully navigating the choppy waters that occur in intimate relationship.

The internet delivers endless sex and dating advice, but there's not a lot of quality education for cultivating presence or authentic communication. It is one thing to find a person to be with, it's an entirely different thing to be with them in a way that consistently brings out the best aspects of each other.

Self-knowledge alone will not get anyone to the Promised Land of Love. My life changed drastically for the better when I took responsibility for my own education with regards to intimate relationship. I hired a relationship coach as a wisdom guide and accountability partner. He was someone who had already traversed the ground I wanted to cross. Our bi-monthly sessions were critical in helping me develop an updated imprint of manhood.

Soul Statement Example
I do not need to be fixed.

Hiring a life coach, attending men's groups and personal development workshops were just initial steps. In order to make real progress, I had to make an ironclad agreement with myself to show up for life no matter what. This meant owning my desire, my mistakes and my *Grrr*. No excuses. One can have excuses or results, but not both.

When I claimed the genuine version of me, I began giving others my presence and my heart over my mind. I discovered that real is preferable to polite. I had to be willing to be less than skillful and fail in my lover's eyes more than a few times in order to improve. My outer life began to shift with my increasing internal connection and claiming my voice in service of the real me. Soul Statements are a key component of maintaining alignment with who and what I am.

Issues and Internal Tension

Relationship issues are not problems, however unskillful handling of relationship issues is definitely a problem. Realize that the problem is never just your partner, but it is often your own inability to sit with tension. A person holds tension by simply allowing emotions to remain without rushing to do anything about them. Relationships are strengthened or weakened in moments of tension.

You'll get into trouble if you cannot effectively cope with internal stress. Tension is one thing, how you handle it is another issue. Don't be left with a reaction you'll be ashamed of. Practice the discipline of letting unhelpful impulses subside without acting on them. Unhelpful impulses are just that (unhelpful).

Too often, people practice the skill of holding tension and offering love or acknowledgement, only to give up after it doesn't produce adequate results in the short term. This is a form of *giving to get*. Don't let your mood dictate your manners.

Feeling badly is not permission to act poorly. Set a behavioral floor for yourself as a non-negotiable standard. You don't have to be awesome all the time, but don't be terrible anytime. Stay in ease if it is your partner who is the one in distress. *"How do you want me to listen and respond right now?"*, can be a very helpful question at these times.

Soul Statement Examples

I'm made of tough stuff and can rise above my surface tension.
I can re-align and center myself right now.

How might your relating change if you go deeper and offer your heart and soul with your beloved instead of talking about surface circumstance or worry. Using a Soul Statement can help stop you from acting out or saying something that you will regret. Remind yourself what you're made of and shift into a better state. Then interact as a more grounded and centered adult.

Personal Journaling Exercise

Do I use complaints as a way to get help or attention?
How attached am I to the complaint of the hour?
Would I be left feeling un-moored without my complaints?
What is my deeper need and is there a more empowering
way to meet that need?

Fold or Feel

When faced with a partner's upset, consciously keep your breath full and your belly and jaw relaxed. Feel an energetic connection from the earth to your center. Stay with your breath and attention and offer love to yourself on the inside while using a Soul Statement. With practice, all of this can happen in seconds. When you are connected to who you are, you're not as threatened by other's evaluations or critiques. You then don't have to be in a rush to discount or correct another person's experience.

Soul Statement Example

My connection to the earth sustains me.

Sometimes you'll be with someone who is spinning up emotionally. In this instance, you might help them work it down by anchoring into what is under their surface distress. You may informally ask them for their version of a Soul Statement.

In practice, this might sound like, *"I get that you are distressed. What is underneath this circumstance?"* or *"This is obviously a big deal. What value of yours isn't being met right now?"*

Personal Journaling Exercise
When do I revert to old patterns?
What is my best 'fearless in the face of distress' posture?

Options Other Than Talking
Talking is not always the best way forward when your beloved partner is in some form of distress. Is your default response attempting to comfort your partner mentally, bodily or via a heart connection? When your partner is recycling a story that feeds their anxiety, perhaps you could serve them best by simply offering a loving embrace.

Soul Statement Examples
I have a compassionate heart.
My companion's upset is not really about me.

Feel deeply of yourself and your personal power. Feel the truth of who and what you are. Bring more of you to the room. Spending time in a self-connection before meeting your lover can be extremely useful. Connect with the energy source deep within you. This is what you want to show up for your partner with.

See if you can marvel at the miracle of this person in front of you. Pay attention to what moves them. You might make it an ongoing practice to silently ask yourself, "*What is the best part of me to offer right now?*"

Model what you wish to receive. If you want depth from your partner, model depth. If you desire more lightness, model that. Slow down. Offer a deeper, more connected version of you. Demonstrate your clarity and remember that you are not here to please or fix anyone else. You serve an intimate partner by remaining sensitive to them while bringing forth the best of you.

Personal Journaling Exercise

Am I as connected to my core serenity as I can be right now? What might I adjust in order to feel more grounded?

Breathe Love In

Your partner will usually NOT react, respond and express like you would in any given instance. That is normal and expected. Their different behavior does NOT make them a defective version of you. It simply means that they have a different history, perception, body and perspective.

Soul Statement Examples

I am complete and valuable.
I am bathed in love.
When in doubt, I can offer my presence.

When feeling the tension level rise (whether theirs or your own), one of the most effective practices is to **simply breathe love in**. This is incredibly useful for when you might otherwise abandon your own heart in the face of hurt. Feel what's under your surface distress.

Can you fill yourself with enough love that you can speak directly to your unmet needs with grace and skill? Can you fill yourself with enough love that you get in touch with what you're willing to give rather than demanding something from your companion?

Soul Statement Examples
I am a loved child of God.
I can breathe love in and feel it calm me.
Love gives me space.

A solution will usually be more obvious when both people feel connected to one another. When you achieve generosity of spirit as a result of real connection, THEN you can explore solution strategies. Oftentimes, connection IS the fix. How might your outcomes change if you built the habit of choosing connection first?

Breathing Love Meditation
Find a comfortable position for your body and close your eyes. Adjust your posture, roll your shoulders, stretch, breath, sigh or yawn as needed to create more ease. Take some time and allow your natural breathing to soften.

Now imagine that every breathable air molecule is imbued with love. Feel love effortlessly entering and filling your lungs and body. Allow this love to animate all of you down to the cellular level.

Breathe into your heart. Gather your essential love energy here. Gently let this love expand and fill the immediate space around your body.

Offer love to wherever it is most needed with your exhalation. Open up to any message of your heart's wisdom as you savor and bask in this light and love

As you breathe in, cherish yourself. As you breathe out,
cherish all beings. ~ His Holiness, The 14th Dalai Lama of Tibet

The Mist (emotionally triggered state / losing perspective)
Communication skills naturally suffer when one is feeling badly. When a person is triggered, their world shrinks down to one priority, which is, *make this unwanted feeling go away!* The only thing that matters in that moment is getting rid of emotional pain and this need blurs all decisions until the triggering subsides.

When a person is triggered into a stress response, the reptilian part of their brain overrides reasonable self-talk. I refer to being triggered in this way as entering **The Mist**. If you've ever been disoriented, completely turned and frustrated around in a dark, foggy night with no sense of the way out, you'll know that it is much like being emotionally triggered.

Common Emotional Triggers
Feeling unheard.
Being interrupted.
Yelling from across the house versus coming closer to speak.
Feeling rushed.

An emotional upset can easily send a person into an old story that will color their perception of what's occurring in present time. People naturally tend to repeat old patterns of behavior during relationship distress. These are often the same behaviors that did not alleviate distress, or serve anyone very well, in the past.

The great challenge for any of us when we're triggered is learning how to find an exit ramp and walk back out of **The Mist** instead of repeating a hurtful behavioral pattern. Feeling emotionally triggered is a warning that one may have bought in to another person's negative story. In this instance, a person has likely forgotten their own lovable-ness.

As soon as you notice the first hint of triggering (unease or a twinge of feeling slighted), ground yourself. Press PAUSE on the voice of your ego and let a Soul Statement guide your mind and heart. Speak to feelings rather than acting them out. Use the following questions to help walk back out of **The Mist** and return to a relational sweet spot.

Sample Questions
Do I have the emotional resources to be present?
What am I feeling and how do I increase my ease?
What would benefit me and my partner most right now?

We all battle the conditioning of our upbringing and previous experience. Patterns are patterns for good reason. If we are not aware of a perfectly good resource then we cannot utilize said resource. Being triggered is a good time to pause with no excuse needed. You may speak something like, "*I need to take a break so that I can be able to take in what you are saying*". Use your time away from the conversation to gather your composure and decide what you want to bring back to the conversation.

Soul Statement Examples (when triggered)
I am love and loved no matter what.
I will never abandon you. (Speak this to your own heart.)
This emotional weather will pass.

I've found it helpful to spend time thinking or journaling about patterns that led to relational distress in the past. Consider that YOU were the common denominator in all your past relationships. Take a look at which unhelpful behavior patterns can be traced back to you. The good news is that, with awareness, you have the power to make changes going forward.

Personal Journaling Exercise

What were my previous partners' main complaints regarding me?

Am I still doing some or all of those things?

What would it take for me to discard one unhelpful behavior?

Slow Down

We can too easily make a partner go from hero to zero in an instant. **The number one skill when emotions flare is being able to slow down**. Slowing down is a skill and can be improved with effort and practice. If you can't find better words in the moment, slow down your speech tempo to increase the likelihood of being heard.

Whenever you first start to feel contracted or distressed is when applying an alternate internal message is most helpful. Pause to notice what is occurring and allow a moment of compassion for your constricted heart. Apply a Soul Statement and shift into a more empowered posture.

This is not theory, but a real way to stop the *misery-go-round* and return to harmonious loving. **Stop** (pause talking). **Drop** (feel your inner constriction and offer self-compassion). **Roll** (act better). **Stop**, Drop and Roll.

A helpful response when feeling triggered is to pause and offer compassion to your wounded ego. Take a few seconds to remember that hurt often comes from an old story or assumption. Hurt also comes from temporarily forgetting one's own loveable-ness. Accept some amount of internal tension and resist the natural impulse to quickly 'fix' feelings.

Ask yourself, *"Am I working this issue (and feelings) up or am I working it down?"*. You can work it down (tap the brakes) by giving acknowledgement and pausing to collect your serenity. Look for positive intent. Don't just listen to your partner's content, feel their heart yearning for something better. Look for the unmet need underneath their words.

I often recall the wise advice of an Outward Bound instructor who said, *"Don't just do something, sit there. Make tea and consider your options"*. This advice means to not rush into doing any old (probably wrong) thing, but consider your challenges and resources regarding the next action. Remember, it always matters what you say to yourself on the inside at the moment of edginess or irritation.

Real-Time Questions
Will my words increase or decrease connection?
Will my actions foster or reduce connection?
I could be easier on my partner by...

The Power of Empathy
We all learned to pay attention to our stomach and bladder. We can also learn to pay attention to our empathy. In a trying situation, BEFORE trying to understand another person's perspective, give yourself empathy. Maintaining a daily self-empathy practice will help make this a natural default.

As soon as distress occurs, drop in and offer silent acknowledgment of what is occurring in your body. Anchor into what is really true so you may engage appropriately rather than run away, shut down or lash out. From a state of self-empathy, you're more resourced. Whether alone or with others, the first step is always the same, and that is to fill yourself with love. Sometimes your emotional well may be full enough that you're able to be an *emotional battery pack* for someone else.

Sometimes I go about pitying myself. And all the while
I am being carried on great winds across the sky.
~ Anonymous (Lakota, 19th century)

When you're *emotionally sunburned*, keep slowing things down. Think Slow to Go. **Speed to empathy is a wonderful contest**! Just touching your beloved in a caring manner or placing your bodies together and breathing can be helpful to restore a feeling of connection and of being on the same team.

Remember that all these various methods and tools work best when you least want to do them. Next time there is relationship tension, observe your response and see if you can shift into a willingness to more skillfully engage and simply embrace what is up.

Soul Statement Examples
Slowing down serves me.
Empathy feels good inside my body.

Beyond Fight or Flight ('F' responses)
Some common human distress responses are; **Fight**, **Flight**, and **Freeze**. Some people's Go-To response is immediately attempting to **Fix** their or the other person's feelings. I do not have judgement about which 'F' word responses a person chooses. We have all done many of them at different stages of our life. The following list is my personal compilation of 'F' words relevant to intimate relationship.

To Fight is meeting opposition with opposition. For example, lashing out at someone when you're offended. Sometimes it can take the form of aggressively building a verbal case against another person. The **Fight** response is often used as a mechanism to avoid being vulnerable. To **Fight** is the opposite of being non-defensive and openhearted. A **Fight** often creates yet more wounding and more of a basis for the next argument.

To Flee (Flight) is to physically or emotionally run away. When confronted with uncomfortable emotions is your default to lean in or to exit in some fashion? This will often trigger feelings of abandonment and lack of safety in the other person. To **Flee** only postpones an inevitable facing of hard truths and associated growth.

Some persons may default to a **Fantasy**. In this instance, a person is not recognizing the difference between a real-life event and a story that is running inside their own head. The version that they are operating from is preferable to facing the truth of how they are actually being treated. Reaching out to neutral allies with a non-defensiveness attitude is one antidote to help overcome a **Fantasy** response.

To Faint (or **Fold**) is to isolate and withdraw from conflict. This may look like a collapse into self-pity or apologizing. We've all seen the person who blames others or external circumstances to validate why they can't take action for themselves. Sometimes this may be due to fear of success. *"What if I stepped up and claimed by bigger life?"*, can be terrifying to answer.

To Freak (or **Flail**) would be to act outrageously and let one's emotions and words get out of control. A person will commonly say something that they will regret (and not be able to take back) when in **Freak** or **Flail** mode. This often throws away accumulated goodwill. We've all seen or done it. It's not pretty.

To Freeze is to become emotionally paralyzed, as in, not knowing what to do or say next and so doing nothing. This can occur when a person has too many choices to sort out easily and so becomes stuck in indecision. It can also occur when you're re-traumatized by a current event. This is one reason that it's wise to have appropriate resources in place ahead of time.

To Fix is a way of trying to make yourself or others feel better. It can be helpful to ask yourself which person is more uncomfortable (you or they). Ask yourself, *"Am I really just trying to make MYSELF"* *feel better by attempting to console this other person?"* **Fixing** can be an attempt to shortcut past an awkward or uncomfortable moment. We all know that shortcuts do not save time or effort in the bigger scheme of things. There is often time for doing nothing about a problem. Giving oneself a respectful pause can allow alternate choices to appear.

To go to Fun is to respond to interpersonal stress by joking, distraction or otherwise making light of something that is worthy of honest attention and dignity. This type of relationship avoidance can feel dishonoring to others. Distraction of this type is often an ego-protection strategy. Honest evaluation of one's own motivation is the remedy for **Fun** as an inappropriate response.

To Feel means to simply be present for the consequences or pain of what has occurred. This involves a commitment to vulnerability and truth, which lowers the emotional wall between people.

When you can identify and communicate your beautiful needs and/or acknowledge someone else's beautiful needs, the connection is strengthened and everyone wins. In the Spanish language, the term for *"I'm sorry"* is *"lo siento"*, which translates as *"I **feel**."* How beautiful and connecting is that?

To **Flow** is to accept life as it comes and allow other people their own pace of personal growth. A person in **Flow** lives life on life's terms and remains open to new perspective and new knowledge. In a **Flow** response one is connected to their soul values and so their composure isn't threatened by upset or distress.

The term **Fuck** need not always have a negative connotation. To **Fuck** in one context is simply to engage life on life's terms, to dive in and 'go for it'. It can represent a fearless attitude of, *"Let's engage with what's real and penetrate the center of what is happening. Let's play in possibility and embrace the texture of what is".* A person who has achieved this relationship with **Fuck** need not apologize for their respectful and true expression.

The first eight 'F' responses in this list are symptomatic of being *off* or not connected with one's own center. The final three 'F' responses in this list are the mark of a more integrated and resourced human being. Connect inwardly and center yourself first so you can act in congruence with the essence of who you are. See if you can choose a more adult 'F' word response when you encounter troubling events going forward.

Spend time with people who model the type of response that you wish to incorporate for yourself. Soul Statements can assist you in building a consistent practice of connecting to your deeper values and needs. **Note**: A good therapist is a sensible choice for up-leveling your default stress response.

Personal Journaling Exercise
Which 'F' word is my default response?
Which 'F' word response would serve me better in heated moments?
Which is my beloved's typical 'F' word stress response?

Freeze or Swing the Bat
I played Little League baseball as a kid. My dad loved the game passionately and taught me true sportsmanship by consistent example. I loved the game, too. However, there was one big problem. When it was my turn at the plate, I would never swing the bat. The pitcher seemed like a daunting opponent and I was paralyzed to act as the ball flew by.

I really wanted to hit the ball. I knew how to swing. I could swing the bat in practice. It's just that when game time came, I froze. The moment of truth found me lacking.

During my last year of baseball, I managed to blindly swing on rare occasion, but there were zero hits. I knew my dad was watching because he was the coach. I knew my dad had been a star player, with lots of athletic trophies, in his day. I knew that a swing was expected. I knew how. I just didn't do it.

Years later I was in a similar-feeling situation whenever I wanted to talk to a girl. I would have imaginary conversations with them in my head. But I didn't step up, take advantage of proximity and begin to talk with a girl during all of high school.

There was one young woman whom I spent time with, but she initiated conversation and so we became decent friends. No romance, just friends. I was wildly attracted to her, but had no concept of how to speak about my desire for more and so I folded time and again.

Soul Statement Example

Swinging the bat serves me and others.

Self-Soothe

We humans tend to fight about our core vulnerabilities. The old saying is true that, *hurt people hurt people*. What if you were able to salve your contracting heart in the moment of wounding (before causing a new wound)? What is at issue is not always expressed with words. What if you had a way to feel love on the inside before responding to an unhappy event?

My coaching clients find it useful to apply a Soul Statement as a way of a diverting stressful thinking into sincere acknowledgment of their true nature. Employing a Soul Statement is a way to remain in an empowered present when you might otherwise abandon your heart.

It is possible to learn how to argue without wounding. I'm an advocate of learning to self-soothe in the moment when an emotional wound is poked. When you recognize that you've just flipped into a poor state, that is a cue to press PAUSE and get your immediate needs met (with as much grace as you can).

Tune inwardly and connect with love. Ground yourself and feel the truth of your being with a Soul Statement. These steps will also help you to hold a better state if it is a partner who is in distress.

Self-soothe tools that I employ are: offering love to whatever disturbs me inside myself, telling myself something true about me (Soul Statement), asking for clarification, making a redo and taking personal space. Stop yourself from attempting to address anything important or that which causes conflict when you're worn down, in a rush or feeling *off*.

Soul Statement Examples
My heart is a jewel and I am lovable.
My heart is beautiful and worthy of expression.
I am more than my thoughts and this too shall pass.

An ongoing self-soothe practice is one ingredient to a life of clarity and ease. In order to access a better state, we have to practice self-soothing before and during an emotionally-triggered state. Self-care after a triggering event has come and gone is second-best.

Poor states lead to poor decisions and poor actions, which have poor consequences. Trying to resolve a troublesome point of contention from a poor state is one way that people get lost in **The Mist** (triggered to the point of losing perspective).

Personal Journaling Exercise
How can I anchor to my highest self in moments of choice?
When will I step up and be more present in situations when
I used to fold?

A structure for *tapping the brakes* is a great item for a relational tool kit. This structure may just be one person saying, *"I'm feeling contracted and a short pause would help me to better hear what you're saying"*. Whatever is said, do it in a manner that maintains respectful connection to your partner.

Soul Statement Example
Love will lead me to my ease.

Emotions are Signals (not enemies)
Emotions are a trustable guide. A strong emotion can alert you to what matters. When experiencing fear, people often freak out and diminish goodwill in order to find an exit ramp from the unwanted feeling. Choosing fearlessness may involve staying with your breath and offering your partner love or some form of acknowledgment when it's most difficult to do so.

Attempting to get rid of fear entirely is a daunting task. Next time fear is threatening to overwhelm you, try and lessen the fear rather than attempt to get away from the fearful state altogether. To *fear less* is a worthy and more achievable goal.

Emotion will move me more than any thought of should or shouldn't. Incoming statements without an emotional cue are often just noise to me. When my partner is in distress, I am affected most when she shares how she's emotionally impacted.

Sharing her relevant emotion gets me to pay attention right away. When you consistently value a partner's emotions, you'll become more intimate and allied as a couple. **Tip**: In terms of an intimate relationship, leave "*why*" questions for a trained therapist.

Danger Signaling (using code words)
Being uncomfortable in your own skin for a bit is okay, but reacting badly is not okay. To avoid reacting badly, many couples employ a system where either person may call a pause with an agreed-upon code word.

For example, the word, "***armchair***", may communicate that a person is becoming agitated and in need of a break. Saying "***armchair***" is a signal for both persons to suspend talking and avoid eye contact while applying self-empathy.

In an ***armchair*** situation, one person might say, *"Even though what you have to say is important, I feel myself contracting so I need an **armchair**."* You may also just say something like, *"I want to hear and appreciate you and I'm having trouble listening right now. Let's pause for just a few moments."*

If a person's (or both person's) emotion or behavior is ramping up further then a stop may be called by employing a different code word. The word, ***apple***, is another code word example. In an ***apple*** situation, one person could say, *"I need to take an **apple** and step away in order to participate in a better fashion later."* This stop may be a physical separation, but not an open-ended abandonment. It's important to agree (prior to separating) on when you'll return. Each person then takes some time to get right with himself or herself.

There is often great benefit in taking a break (especially when words are the cause of more wounding). Use the separation as a time to look into your own motivation or imagine how your words and actions may have felt to the other person.

Depending on the length of separation, this may be done with friends, a therapist, in nature, the gym or with your Higher Power. Do what it takes to return to a centered and grounded state. Return at the agreed-upon time with broader perspective and a re-filled emotional well.

Pain is Valid

Most interpersonal fights are essentially arguing for whose pain is greater. If you cannot accept the other person's painful experience as valid and real for them, then the relationship is on shaky ground. Self-soothe as needed to gain the ability to remain present and hold a measure of empathic listening.

A normal human response is to want the person perceived as hurting you to be the source of a solution and to want your wound solved or salved by them immediately. It is not a great formula to look for happiness in the same place that you lost it.

When there is distress in another person, begin with deep listening. The more you and a partner see and accept each other's experience, the more you'll uncover mutuality. You might lead off sharing an upset with something like the following, *"Something is up for me and you're not wrong. Do you have space to listen for a few minutes?"*. This is easier to hear than, *"I'm upset and need to talk right freakin' now!"*. Make it a discipline to choose empathic listening and *hear what hurts* the other person.

Self-Improvement Challenge
Can you accept your partner's unfiltered displeasure
without losing your poise?

Your thoughts and actions are most definitely your responsibility. Understanding the impact of your actions is critical because this is what can move you to be better. Achieving an understanding of another person's distress on a mental level won't always translate into behavior change. Allowing another person's pain to land on your heart is more likely to result in better actions going forward.

Soul Statement Example
My wounded ego does not diminish the strength of my heart.

Conflict Done Well Can Lead You Home
Allowing conflict to help discover a place of openness and depth is very possible. This is because a beautiful, raw state done well can facilitate honesty and vulnerability. If you can find a way to be connected to your center in those moments of distress, you can trade tension for empathy. Connection and acceptable solutions then become more attainable.

Sharing mistrust can become a source of trust if both parties are able to drop into vulnerability and openheartedness. After a difficult sharing people often find it helpful to just sit and let the empathy steep. Judith Orloff, MD and others call this, *"empath-tea"* (which I love). Actually ask yourself this question: *"Can I sit and let the empath-tea steep?"*.

Teasing is Poor Practice

A poor pattern that I once had was to tease my intimate companion. The urge to tease suppresses movement toward depth and creates confusion for the other person. As an example, years ago I found an unused condom in my girlfriend's car. We both had clean STI tests and so didn't use them.

We both had permission to cuddle with other friends, but nothing that needed a condom. Her flippant, joking answer put me off. It did not occur to her that she would ever violate my trust and so she thought a joke was alright. Although I knew she embodied integrity, I did not need this confusion in my heart.

I have since made teasing off-limits for myself. Now, when I feel the urge to tease my intimate partner, I stop myself. With a rare teasing slip, I might say, *"In the interest of establishing a new pattern I'd like to redo what I just said"*.

Soul Statement Example

There is a beautiful need underneath my impulse to tease.

Chapter Summary

Activate a Soul Statement to support the discipline of letting unhelpful impulses subside without acting on them. Feeling bad is not permission to act poorly. Learn to be with tension rather than rush to feel better. Do what you must to shift into a better state. Breathe in love and offer truth and depth to your beloved companion. Utilize a code word as needed.

Employing self-empathy and an attitude of undefended honesty underneath the various practices and tools is key to better navigating **The Mist**. Press PAUSE on the voice of your ego and let a Soul Statement guide your mind and heart. Speak to feelings rather than acting them out. If you want depth, model depth. If you desire more lightness, model lightness.

In a trying situation, BEFORE trying to understand another person's perspective, give yourself empathy. Make it a strict discipline to choose empathic listening and *hear what hurts*. Accept your partner's experience as valid. Speed to empathy is a wonderful contest!

Conflict doesn't always have to lead to more conflict. When you emphasize connection, conflict can become a stepping-stone to more intimacy.

In the next chapter, we'll discover more about how to amplify the appreciation that one brings to a beloved partner. We'll present the beautiful practice of a **Heart Hello**.

We'll go further into the importance of physical intimacy along with benefits of living in wonder and of having a *giraffe* friend.

If you are moved to, tag me in a social media post about how you're rising above internal tension and/or choosing an upgraded F-response, with the hashtags #empathymatters #betterself

I I

INTIMATE RELATIONSHIP HARMONY

I slept and dreamt that life was joy. I awoke and saw that
life was service. I acted and, behold, service was joy.
~ Rabindranath Tagore

My beloved is truth. She is truth because she's connected to her heart and to the flow of spirit. She is love at her core. She is a living feminine force as manifested as a natural play of light. I constantly benefit from the real-time example of radiance and shifting expression she offers. I remain a student of her and I am keenly aware that I will never fully know her. I do, however, want to be the world's leading authority on how to best love this person.

Soul Statement Example

I am strong in my center.

Ideally, you want your partner to have a good time by being with you. That being said, you don't serve anyone by attempting to analyze or solve their feelings. It is not an appropriate relationship role to tailgate a partner's ever-changing texture of emotion. Help your partner by simply breathing into your center and feel a measure of lightness. Use a Soul Statement as needed to connect your sure center to your surface mind.

How you show up for your partner is need-to-know information if you wish to serve love and grow into your power. Suspend your ego in order to understand your impact versus arguing for the validity of your own experience.

Excelling at self-correction is linked to a commitment to hearing difficult feedback. Do your feelings have to be salved or does hard information need to be sugar-coated for you? I'm generally open to hearing if I've I drifted off my grounded center so that I can do what it takes to find the real Corey again.

Soul Statement Example

My center informs me as I love my partner.

A beloved companion will often feel you slip away from your groundedness before you notice yourself doing so. I'm not saying to be overly interested in another's evaluation of your actions, but you may be well-served to welcome their bio-emotional, real-time feedback. It is a gift when your partner reveals their feelings to you. **Remember**: A spoken expression of emotion is a cue to pay attention.

Non-defensiveness is a relationship meta-skill. Your intimate partner is a muse in which you can see the effect of your actions.

Truthful reflection is invaluable if you're interested in growing as a person.

Your commitment to living in truth will help your chosen beloved bring you their joy or anxiety in real time. Of course, you'll do what you must in order to stay grounded. A Soul Statement is like an arrow to the bullseye of what you are really about. It aligns you to your values. Self-connectedness must always be the center around which you organize yourself.

Soul Statement Example

I am served by knowing my truth.

Focus on Feelings and Needs

In my coaching practice, I encourage people to lead conversations with feelings and needs rather than a desired outcome. The story of what occurred is easy to argue about. Feelings are not so arguable. Non-Violent Communication (NVC) teaches that feelings are always connected to needs and values.

Be committed to discovering what matters to your companion. Honor whatever feelings come up when values or needs are not met. Let go of logic and just be with each other. Give people the respect of their own sovereignty and allow them to navigate emotional obstacles in their own fashion and timing. If we make a habit of fixing another person's feelings sooner or later our reward is resentment.

Soul Statement Example

I value and respect my sovereignty.

Surrender to the gift of letting other people have their own pace of development. That is between them and God. (**Translation:** None of your business.) By making your intimate partner's feelings truly important, your brain will send an alert when it hears words like, "contracted, uneasy, tender or open." This internal brain alert should be something like, "*This is important. Pay attention.*" When your partner speaks a feeling word, that's a cue to listen acutely to what comes directly after.

Honor These Signals
Feminine Red Alert: "*I have feelings.*"
Masculine Red Alert: "*I'm hungry.*"

Keeping a Light Heart
It is lightheartedness in the face of opposition or adversity that lets another person trust that you will hold up your side of the relationship. Don't crumble into self-pity in an attempt to salve your own internal tension.

Don't allow a companion's wild emotions to spin you into an impossible vortex of feelings. Aspire to be the person who can simply hear criticism and not succumb to defensiveness or drama. Let any reactivity to be a signal to do some inner adjustment.

When you honor emotions, you don't have to be consumed by them, but can let them inform your next action. Soul Statements can improve and enhance intimate relationship harmony by helping each person identify and speak to what is true in their heart versus forming a complaint. During times of strain a Soul Statement can help you work through trouble.

Soul Statement Examples
I can and will get through this.
I am more than strong enough.

Stepping Up

Rather than re-fighting a past relationship battle, be interested in engaging deeply with a present distress or disturbance in order to find your way back to alignment and harmony. Make it a goal to simply learn more about what moves and affects your partner. Regularly re-anchor to the reasons you and your beloved are together.

Consider any intimate companion as a blessing of light in your life. Realize that your partner is giving you his/her/their most sacred and precious possession, which is time. Neither you nor they were drafted for the position of beloved. You each volunteered and need not remain if the situation becomes untenable.

This person is not obligated to put up with any situation or behavior that makes them uncomfortable or unhappy. Hold the attitude that they (not you) are the most important person in the room. Re-visiting this perspective helps restore appreciation for the exquisiteness of your time together.

Soul Statements and consistent activities that anchor you to your core enhance the ability to consistently show up as the best version of you. Remember to practice the meta-skill of holding your own tension in order to really listen to your partner.

If unsure of what your partner is needing, you might say, *"Is this something that you want help finding a solution to or do you just want me to listen right now?"*. Do whatever it takes to simply listen and learn. **Note:** You'll increase personal happiness just by stepping up and acting better.

Soul Statement Example

My emotions are a superpower.

Your partner is not a problem in need of repair. Consider that they are more like an endlessly unfolding treasure-puzzle. If you cannot articulate why you're with a beloved, spend some solo time to gain clarity on the purpose of your participation in the relationship.

Your partner's spiritual and emotional health is sacred and sovereign. They add grace to your life by being in it. You are spiritual mirrors for each other. Generally, each person will present lessons and challenges that the other person is in need of in order to grow. The interplay of friendship and togetherness in intimacy is an ongoing learning.

Ask yourself what you really want in your intimate relating. What are your deal-killers? Do your values align with the values of the person you're with? Discover where your values and needs overlap with your partner and where they don't.

You may both want to journal a list of qualities that you love and treasure about the other person and then share the lists with each other. Make this a basis for a truth-telling conversation.

Bringing distress or difficulty to one's partner with grace and kindness can engender trust and lead to deeper connection. It is a beautiful feeling to know that either of you can bring up any issue or awkwardness and you'll hold each other with love, patience and generous hearts.

Speak to your unwanted feelings versus acting them out. Find the place in your heart where lives the desire to love and support your beloved. It is lovely to offer (and to hear), *"I acknowledge your hurt and I am committed to loving you and learning how to be a better partner."*

Non-Defensiveness Challenge

Make it a discipline to not defend your thoughts or actions
for 10 days.
Listen to external feedback and process it internally with
strict honesty.
Remain in a 'listen and learn' mode.

Mutual understanding comes more readily when you're connected to how you really feel and who you are to each other in the bigger picture. From a place of connection and caring two persons can more easily arrive at a mutual strategy for harmony. Listen to the other person, but don't just hear their words as information. Let whatever is expressed land on your heart. Offer empathy, or at least acknowledgement, before proceeding. Let this process be one of loving discovery.

Soul Statement Example
I can touch the love at my core.

Avoid dragging your lovely partner through the muddy neighborhood that is your insecurity and petty struggle. It's generally better to process your troubles with a neutral third party and then bring newfound clarity and sureness back to your beloved. Do what you must to uncover the needs beneath your wants.

When you're together, aim to arrive at the sweet spot where both persons are non-defensive and get what's alive for the other person. Doing this process with the guidance of a trusted therapist would typically help get you to a better place more quickly and easily than attempting this on your own.

Soul Statement Examples
I am openhearted and care about others.
I am secure enough to admit a mis-step.

When trying to work out an emotionally sticky issue with a beloved partner, the internal conversation can become, *"What am I willing to give?"* rather than, *"What am I willing to give up?"*. One way to help get there is to keep acknowledging each other and to keep returning to empathy.

Don't offer solutions until the other person is ready to hear your ideas. When each of you feel heard, acknowledged and complete, THEN you can talk about solutions. It is better to be a solution-rather than a problem-solver, but skipping ahead to a solution can feel dishonoring of hurt feelings.

During times of relationship distress, go deep. When the situation isn't easy, that is the time to act better. Offer something other than words from your thinking mind. Slow down into deep presence by first connecting to your body, heart and soul. Think not about pleasing anyone else, rather focus on opening to a direct experience of love. **A good maxim**: *Give a bit of your heart rather than a piece of your mind.*

Before marriage keep your eyes wide open.
Afterwards, half shut. ~ Benjamin Franklin

Non-Violent Communication (NVC) teaches that a primary commitment should be to the *quality of communication*. Rather than argue for why you did this or that, simply listen to your companion. Get the impact of what he/she/they experienced from the actions you did or didn't do.

You will move closer to relationship harmony when you can deepen your attention and accept the experience of others. Actively choose to practice kindness. Consistently holding kindness as a high value for yourself allows for greater ease navigating relational rough patches. **Remember**: Kindness works its magic best when you least want to offer it.

Values Alignment Exercise

Make a list with these headings; sleep, music, recreation, sex, food, spiritual practice, mental stimulation, social interaction, alone time, exercise, life goals, daily schedule, financial priorities and goals, geography, fun activities, vacations...

Write your specific needs, desires, timing, etc. under each heading. You may also make note of the relevant value that would be met alongside a given item. Now assign one of these priority levels to each specific item on your list as follows:

Must experience often.

Would really like with some frequency.

Would be nice to experience now and then.

Won't do or won't put up with.

You may use this process to see where your life and intimate relationship could improve. Ideally, both partners would create their own list to be shared with each other as the basis for a truth-telling and solution-finding conversation.

Appreciation and Trust

I believe that anyone will benefit from a feminine partner's perspective if they are open to trusting her gifts and earnest about learning what moves her. Let your starting point be caring about her experience. I operate from the attitude that my basic job in intimate relationship is to be in a state of appreciation for my feminine partner.

A feminine-aligned person naturally senses currents of energy that a masculine-aligned person may only dimly perceive. Consider that a feminine-aligned person has ever-changing sensitivity and perception. It often seems that my woman is following invisible spirit trails that I will never see. So, I sometimes act as if walking past a ceremony in progress when I see her absorbed in something.

Appreciation Diet

Many people have amazing results by performing a 30-day diet of appreciation. Simply, substitute an appreciation in your mind every time you hear a critical thought regarding your partner. Only allow appreciations for your partner to come out of your mouth for the month. **Pro version**: With each slip, the 30-day clock starts over at the beginning.

Love Letter Exercise

Write a letter to your beloved describing in great detail how you see him/her/they and how the relationship inspires you. Keep this letter on your personal altar or in a treasure box. Write out another copy and send it in the mail to your beloved.

Heart Hello

A personalized **Heart Hello** is simply a semi-formal, intentional hello, perhaps with the attitude of, *"Let me see God in you"*, that one can share with a beloved. A **Heart Hello** can be made in seconds and is an easy way to re-orient to love. It can be as simple as, *"Hello friend. I'm so happy to be on this journey with you."* Acknowledge the shared connection and offer the best of yourself for this brief moment. Offer love with your eyes, words, touch and/or speech.

For the duration of the **Heart Hello**, get out of your head. The conversation in there will be available later. Meanwhile, you have just made a difference for each other. You might briefly speak a Soul Statement or say what you are for each other at this time. This is a lot like giving a houseplant a drink of water. Plants and people do best with a small amount of nourishment fairly often and a larger drink every once in a while.

You might enroll your partner for a **Heart Hello** practice by saying something like, *"In the interest of enhancing our love, I'd like to take an extra few seconds to connect at transitions."* Slow down, increase your love-energy and the moment can become a sweet hello at transitions or whenever the spirit moves you. Appropriate times could be: leaving the house, arriving home, mealtime, just before sleep and upon waking. Think **Stop, Pause, Connect**. Do this consistently for a week and watch intimacy blossom!

A **Heart Hello** can include an energetically-clean hug with no obligation to do more. When you're in closer energetic harmony it is easier to move to greater intimacy or you may just allow the loving touch to be a renewing contact. Share the space between you rather than occupying it all yourself.

Over-merging with another person reduces sexual charge. You don't want to surround yourself with a thick energetic barrier at one extreme, but giving your all while holding nothing back for yourself is unappealing.

You give a partner the best of you when you rest in the center of your heart and allow a higher love to shine through. It is your steady, clear, contained presence that others desire most. Putting your bodies together in a centered way will usually shift both of you in a good direction. Specific appreciations that are spoken out loud keep love and goodwill front and center.

Reminding yourself of what you admire about your partner is an antidote to feeling ungrateful. Create a **Heart Hello** or speak appreciations in the flow of conversation. The feminine is buoyed with affirmation that love is present, so why hold back? The tantra teacher, Charles Muir says, *"Begin and end every day with love."*

Soul Statement Examples
My happiness increases when I show up and act better.
My happiness increases when I step up.
I get to design my experience of life.

Words That You've Always Wanted To Hear
I really like the practice of asking for what you most crave to hear. Perhaps there are some words that you have always wanted to hear someone say to you?

If so, ask your beloved partner if they are willing to look you in the eyes and say those actual words out loud. If they're willing, then sit knee-to-knee, relax and breathe together. When you feel ready, signal your partner and then allow their spoken words to land inside you.

Some examples that people have found impactful include: "*I trust you*", "*I want you*" and "*I admire you*". You might simply respond with, "*thank you*" or "*I believe you*" as you allow the words to land on your heart. Give yourself permission to believe what you are hearing. Resist the temptation to distract yourself from accepting and feeling this beautiful sentiment fully.

Personal Journaling Exercise
What I've always wanted to hear an intimate partner say to me is...
What I need in order to be able to ask for this is...

This does not have to be a one-off event. Ask your partner to say the words a few times in order to feel the emotional impact more and more deeply. When one's heart is vulnerable and undefended, such as in lovemaking, is a nice time to imprint the feeling of affirming words. Return to this practice as desired and notice how your requests change.

Pre-Flight Checklist
You may find a personal check-in useful before meeting up
with an intimate partner. Here is one that I used for years:

Be rested and relaxed.
Take a quiet moment to feel stillness my center.
Know what I am bringing.
How can I add light to our experience?
Check the careful guy at the door.

Physical Intimacy is Important
One of my failings in past relationships was not insisting on time for
physical intimacy on a regular basis. Making and keeping intimate
dates helps cement a sacred contract to love and to loving. Whether
consciously or not, your partner wants to feel that your love is a
constant.

Physical intimacy anchors a couple to the reason they are together
and harmonizes their nervous systems. Lovemaking is a chance to
see each other in the best light – anchored in your highest self and
offering hyper-present expression in real time. Why not choose to
see each other as god and goddess while making love? Lovemaking
after a tense time can be incredible experience of vulnerability,
tenderness and healing. Making love is not a euphemism!

Soul Statement Examples
I am made in God's likeness.
I have a sacred contract to love and to loving.

One way to approach closeness after an intimacy drought is with
no-obligation and no-implication touch. Too often, people don't
touch their partner when they're not up for sexual intercourse and
so are over-cautious about how loving touch might be perceived. It

may be that they don't trust their own ability to verbally tap the brakes or they want to avoid an emotional minefield if an, *"I'm not up for more right now"* is not accepted graciously.

No-obligation / no-implication touch allows people to be free to make physical contact without pressure to do more. Tell your partner that you'd like to touch and be touched in a way that doesn't always lead to penetrative sex.

Perhaps, take sex off the table unless asked for and formally consented to. Use your voice when you're up for more and when you're not. If you can trust yourself to use your voice, then more freedom and choices open up.

Loving touch is an essential emotional nutrient. A hand on the shoulder or neck can feel affirming and add to the enjoyment of a day. I call loving touch, ***Vitamin T.*** I had a lover who often asked, *"Could we just hold each other?"*. This was much better than if she had held back from voicing her needs and only got physically held during *official* lovemaking.

This request may also be phrased as, *"I want to deepen our connection, could we just pause and be together without talking right now?"*. Physical affection gives a direct transmission that you're here and you want each other. Touch your beloved often.

Personal Journaling Exercise
Is my Vitamin T level optimal or not?
What requests could I make to increase my Vitamin T?

I'm a big fan of lying together in a spooning position. Have the person who feels more needy or vulnerable in front. This is truly amazing for harmonizing a couple's energy. You can also take spooning up a level with intentional breathing. The person who is behind breathes (calmly) near enough to the other person's ear that they may breathe in unison.

Consider S.E.X. as standing for **Sacred Energy eXchange**. Sex is sacred as we declare it to be so. Hold sexual union as a holy sacrament in your heart. Conscious Sexuality is an invitation to reconcile one's spirituality and sexuality. Lovemaking is often when people re-remember why they enjoy being together. Bring the perspective and attitude of **Sacred Energy eXchange** to your intimate time and notice what shifts.

Sacred union (spiritual-sexual) experiences give a couple anchor points to remember who and what they are for each other. The feminine partner expressing her own radiant happiness can light up her companion more than any particular action will. A masculine partner secure in his grounded presence allows for deeper trust and openness.

Practice the art of removing any markers from your sexual play except for the quality of joy that you feel in the moment. This change alone might transform your sexing.

A wonderful approach to lovemaking is, **sex without goalposts**. This refers to being in intimate physical play without an orgasm agenda or other finish line. There is no *scoring*. Just have the attitude of being happy to play and connect. Don't do any action in order to get *something better*. Having no time-pressure is its own reward. Let the texture of the moment be enough. **Tantric secret**: *Stillness contains more pleasure than movement.*

What's the usual shape of your body during lovemaking? What would your sexing avatar look like? Are you more of a contorted squirrel or like a mountain lion bounding through snow? During lovemaking, consciously practice softening and opening your body.

When you physically relax and open, the heart will follow. Focus on your quality of attention. Inhabit the moment fully. Find the moment and you'll find rich texture and flavor. Find the moment and you'll step outside of time. Isn't that a wonderful goal to aspire to?

Tantric Lovemaking Practice

How slow can I go?

How deep can I glow?

Can my body and mind stay relaxed and open?

What does your sexing sound like? Is it quiet until approaching climax? Do you make more noise at the dinner table than you do in the bedroom? Do you offer praise and appreciation to your lover? Are you asking for what you want? Are your movements congruent with your emotions?

I encourage you to experiment with sound during sex. Add sound to your emotion. Some couples enjoy sitting knee-to-knee to hum or chant together in order to align their shared field. If you don't know where to begin, the tantra teacher, Charles Muir, says, *"Just pick a vowel."*

Note: Humming higher notes opens your heart. Humming lower notes accesses your deeper *Grrr*. Utilize a Soul Statement as needed to access a more powerful version of you.

The character, Don Juan de Marco, (in the movie of the same name) said, *"Nothing is more important than love."* In tantra we learn to not put off joining in love-play until each person feels sexy. Rather, we utilize sacred love to restore and strengthen harmonious connection.

Slowing down and incorporating beautiful ritual enhances the spiritual aspect of lovemaking. Eye-gazing is a way to go deep with another person in a short time and is an amazing stand-alone experience. All that is required is to simply express caring via the eyes.

Many couples enjoy eye-gazing as a prelude to lovemaking. Remember that your partner wants to feel your essence and your here-and-now love. This is not meant to sound like work. Remain in your grounded ease. Simply transmit love and light when looking at and touching your partner.

Too much of the time, people are boxed into narrow physical expression and it is sex or nothing, and nothing often prevails. This leads to sexual hunger and goal-oriented sex. You may want to enlist the help of a sex therapist, certified tantra educator, love coach or cuddle party facilitator to explore expanded intimacy options.

Living in Wonder

There is great benefit to living in wonder with your partner. What if being present for wonder was your primary job? What would shift if you lived in a state of newness and learning with this person? Beginner's Mind allows one to be more open to learning. When in a state of Beginner's Mind your life flows more easily.

Music carried us along the line of dance as my tango partner matched me step for step and turn for turn. With a hand on her back, I could easily sense when she felt the beginning thought of a turn or stop. She responded in perfect sync to my subtle shifts of weight and posture as she registered the movements in her body. My shoulders shifted only to the extent that I needed her to align with me.

The distance between us was a constant. She allowed me to navigate us safely and smoothly through the crowded dance floor. The music seemed to move us along as one dual-body being. There was no thought chatter or concern. There was no past and no future. We were just dancing. We floated together in this perfect moment.

Tango dancing has been described as vertical lovemaking. Tango dance, done well, is a wonderful example of respect, consent, harmonious union and flow. The dance of tango with its complete attention to nuanced movement is a nice model for sexing.

Tango demands moment-to-moment presence (as should sexual union). This is in contrast to striving and busy-ness, which does not serve physical intimacy. When you achieve a state of wonder for this unique being that chooses you to spend time with and can flow with each other, you both win.

Soul Statement Example
Living in wonder is a gift and a joy.

Your mind is more serene when you're in touch with your true nature. Aspire to find delight and wonder in challenging moments with your beloved. A beloved needs you to be informed from your core essence more than they need what's in your mind.

This other person is a child of God and worthy of understanding (not just during fun and easy moments). If you can see them through a lens of love, great insight and depth may be your reward. Make this perspective a gyroscope that keeps your relationship on its axis.

By keeping one's feelings secret, a beloved partner has to guess what and who they are to you. Voice tone, eye contact, smiles, praise, notes, messages, plans and touch can all demonstrate affection and maintain aliveness. The important thing is to keep orienting to love. Find out your partner's primary, preferred way to receive love and act accordingly. Discover and communicate your own preferences for loving.

Employ a Soul Statement and other tools to return to your center for nourishment and to re-charge your energetic batteries in order to communicate what you really need and want. This way you can show up with greater presence and have something of more substance to offer your chosen beloved (and the greater world).

Soul Statement Examples (for romantic feelings)
The deepest part of me is madly in love with you.
My whole body says, "Yes!" to you.

Giraffes

Giraffe is a term used in Non-Violent Communication (NVC) to indicate a person with a higher perspective that will hold space and listen to you with compassion and presence (especially when you're in distress). This person is not a doormat for drama, but a neutral friend who can lend an ear or more.

Not getting a certain emotional or social need met is much like a vitamin deficiency. After enough time the deficiency affects you to where you need to boost it back up. Having *giraffe* friends is important in order to meet a larger galaxy of needs.

Your intimate partner is generally not the best choice of person with whom to unload fears and insecurities. Identify and spend time with your *giraffes*, people who will meet you in authentic presence and deep listening.

Having a friend other than your primary partner to share difficult issues with means that you don't have to trouble that person with every up and down of your internal process. Having other people to do fun activities with doesn't confine you to activities and times that are good for just one person.

There is benefit to having *giraffes* all along the spectrum of intimacy. Your friendship constellation should ideally be complex enough that there are choices of persons to spend time with depending on what will feed your spirit. This way you may find someone to be a neutral sounding board or a playmate for however deep or light you wish to be on a given day.

Some persons can offer listening at your distressing times. Perhaps you have a trusted peer whom you can run ideas by and they will tell you what they really think. Further along the spectrum is a person you can share more vulnerable issues with and they can hold bigger emotions and venting in confidence.

Still others may be willing to welcome you with cuddling or holding when words are not what helps. An ongoing conversation with your primary beloved will help keep you in integrity with outside interactions.

Personal Journaling Exercise
Needs that I want to find within my primary intimate relationship are...
Needs that are appropriate to find outside my primary intimate relationship are...
What community relationships could I cultivate to round out my 'needs galaxy'?
Who could be a giraffe for me?
Am I a giraffe for anyone (and is this appropriate)?

I want to note that a *giraffe*, or any friend, should, ideally, not just be a 'needs-meeting-only entity', but a co-creator of experience. (The interactions can be unequal at times as long as the scales do tip back to balance.) Know if you are *clinging* or *bringing*. Ask, "*What can I offer this person?*". When in doubt, ask them what their needs are.

When it comes to sharing relationship troubles, it is a respectful choice to vent with a *giraffe* or someone who is grounded and neutral and who will give you honest feedback as opposed to a friend whom both of you have in common. Sharing disharmony with common friends often places them in an awkward situation and increases the likelihood of private information spreading to a greater circle of people.

Up the Feeling of You
Love will find you if you find you first. You attract what you believe you deserve. When you know yourself internally as love, you experience love externally. No one wants to be around a *hungry ghost*. A *hungry ghost* being the person that's looking outside themselves to fill an internal void.

Over time, no one will treat you better than you treat yourself. A good place to begin is to **up-level the feeling of you**. Can you bring more of you to this moment ...and to the next moment? Consistently dial up your presence by just one or two percent and notice how the world responds differently.

Do what you did in the beginning (of the togetherness)
at the end and there won't be an end. ~ Tony Robbins

Chapter Summary

Be committed to non-defensiveness. Trading truth for comfort is a poor bargain. Become willing to hear criticism without succumbing to defensiveness or drama.

Let reactivity be a signal to do some inner adjustment. Use Soul Statements to help you keep a light heart in the face of opposition or adversity.

Ask yourself what you really want in your intimate relationships. Discover where your values and needs overlap with your partner and where they don't.

Don't hold back love. Be creative and make a **Heart Hello** every day. Make requests as needed to increase your *Vitamin T*. Let your sexing become sacred and holy.

Call a *giraffe* as needed. Live in wonder and wonder will seek you out.

In the next chapter, we'll see how clarity and transparency are sexy and how embracing truth allows for living into a greater purpose and to more powerfully serve life.

If you are moved to, tag me in a social media post making a commitment to living in wonder and with a light heart, with the hashtags #livinginwonder #thisisme

I2

LIVING IN INTEGRITY

You get there by realizing you are already there. ~ Eckhart Tolle

As a spark of divine light, who are you to cover up your light and deny it to the world? A Soul Statement allows you to hold the world and your place in it more lightly, while remaining in touch with your deeper presence and values. The next right action is obvious when you're deeply connected to yourself and certain of what you value. You maintain your highest values by living them.

Soul Statement Example
I am valuable and worthy of a place in this world.

A Soul Statement gives you access to an internal reservoir of strength and certitude. Making contact with your true essence in this way will allow you to act from a deeper, informed place. You have more to offer life when you know who and what you are. This place is aspirational AND in your possession now.

187

Trust that life will deliver what you need to grow as a person. When you trust beyond outcome or income you free up your energy and perception to be open to reality as it presents itself. Let go of your unease about past missteps.

The truth is that you were operating from outdated beliefs. Reframe an internal message of being hard on yourself to realize that your behavior arose out of a desire for a better experience. Practice eagerness for life as it unfolds.

Soul Statement Examples
The deep me is the real me.
The deep me is eager for life.
My integrity creates satisfaction.

Just like the film characters, Billy Jack and Luke Skywalker, who each had to enter a dark cave to discover what they were made of, so must each one of us gather courage to visit our own dark passages.

Willingness to tolerate discomfort is a pre-requisite in order to stretch and grow. Admitting one's motivation for a given action is where it gets real. This admission is how you come face-to-face with darker impulses and fears. Owning your fears is how one begins to not be controlled by them.

As I've written earlier, the nice person is simply not alive enough. Be the most fearless version of you. Clarity and transparency are sexy. You don't want an intimate companion to judge that you're *metering* your passion.

Many people reserve their animal expression for the bedroom or the sports playing field. It is good to have appropriate outlets for feeling your *Grrr* outside of those arenas. Remember, the safe person is not the one with zero needs. Let the aliveness inside you spill over a bit... and then a bit more. Boundaries and edges are attractive!

If you are irritated by every rub,
how will your mirror be polished? ~ Rumi

One antidote to living as overly reserved is to push your edge. Being committed to hearing hard or tender truth is foundational to non-defensiveness. Holding back truth from oneself or others creates tension and incongruency. Make the choice to show up as the person you ideally want to be in a given situation.

We've all felt that twinge inside when we hear a necessary truth that we hadn't yet admitted to ourselves. Perhaps we metaphorically sailed unaware past some rocky shoals and even increased our speed until whammo! – we abruptly slammed into a hard life lesson. We've asked, "*Why was this so hard?*".

Consider that the lesson may have been a rough one because smaller nudges were discounted and bypassed along the way. If you're hearing feedback that you don't like, consider that you may be in the right place in order to grow.

Personally, I want to hear feedback that is direct enough to shift me out of complacency. Sometimes, I must claim my inner warrior and be willing to die to an old way of being in order to win the day. Sometimes it is beneficial to say, "*screw politeness*" and own one's genuine expression. I encourage you to take a stand for your desires in an empowering and respectful manner.

Soul Statement Examples

I can trust my deep knowing to guide me.
Truth and transparency serve me.

Due to an ocean-event injury years ago, it is painful for me to sit upright for long periods of time. One summer, I was asked to be a singer at a traditional Native American Sun Dance ceremony. This meant sitting in a chair from before sunrise, whilst drumming and singing most of the day, for four consecutive days. When I accepted the invitation to participate, I imagined myself taking rest breaks as needed.

What actually happened was that I became immersed in the spirit of the ceremony. I was humbled and inspired by the prayers and steadfastness of the dancers and the selfless attitude of the helpers and supporters.

I was uplifted by the prayer songs and by the shimmering beauty of the central tree with its colorful prayer ties. I had no need for rest breaks. My back didn't offer a complaint the entire time. By serving a higher purpose I was allowed to transcend my human frailty.

I meditate on the following archetypal value statement:
I am a warrior scout, master of my body, tuned to
the natural world, committed to winning the day
and aware of the impermanence of this dream.
I'm living in service to my deep expression,
to the divine feminine, to my family and to my tribe.

Personal Journaling Exercise
Write a value statement with archetypes and abilities
that resonate for you.

Keep Going
One early May weekend I awoke before dawn and drove up the nearby mountain road for a solo summit ascent. (At 12,645-feet above sea level, the peak towered 8,600 feet above our tiny town.) I drove until the road became dirt and then parked where the road was blocked by snow.

As the stars faded with the coming light, I set off through the aromatic, dark spruce forest on skis. After the trees thinned out, I tied the skis on my backpack and trudged upward.

The higher I climbed, the steeper the mountain slope became. The tall skis made my pack top-heavy and so keeping my balance was its own challenge. I made slow and tiring progress, but couldn't stop as the sun was quickly warming and softening the snow. Evidence of several point-type avalanches from the previous afternoon were to the right and left of me.

The effort of climbing was relentless and my heart rate soared, so I focused on controlling my breathing. At two-thirds of the way up I was nearing physical exhaustion. I was also very cognizant that I'd lost my best friend to an avalanche on the other side of this same mountain the previous year.

Every step put me a bit higher, but each step was a little steeper than the last and the air was warming by the half-minute. The entire snow slope that I was on was going to slide out from underneath me very soon. I now hit the limit of my physical stamina, but couldn't pause in the death zone. Even if I kept up my progress, I might not make the summit in time.

My options were rest and drastically increase my chance of getting swept to the rock talus 1,800 feet below (sure death) or punch another boot into the snow, step up, re-plant my ice axe, take a deep breath and repeat.

The snow layer became so thin that the pick of my ice axe was hitting rock and I still had sixty vertical feet to go. I was acutely aware of the precariousness of my position, but could not afford to weaken my focus. I simply had to keep moving. I had not anticipated a near vertical climb. Photos of mountaineers in Rock & Ice magazine doing this sort of this thing are amazing, but the doing of it is not fully describable.

Now I was forty feet from the top, then thirty feet. When only twenty feet remained, the danger had not diminished. I was relieved that the typical snow cornice at the top was minimal as I did not have an energy reserve to tackle a wall of overhanging snow. The outcome was not certain until the moment that I stepped onto the level, windswept ground of the mountaintop.

I let my breathing and heart rate subside now that was alone on the high summit with a hundred-mile-plus, 360-degree view. I could see Mt. Tukuhnikivatz, Arches National Park, Klondike Bluffs, the Roan and Book Cliffs, the Abajos and Henry Mountains, Back of Beyond, San Rafael Swell, Island in the Sky, Needles District, Dolores River Canyon, Uncompahgre Plateau, Lone Cone, Sleeping Ute, the La Plata peaks and more. I was in love with all the country within my vision.

After resting, I took a 'relatively' safe route down a rocky knife ridge and eventually skied through the forest to my vehicle. I had dug deep, and deeper still, and kept moving when it was most difficult to do so.

I fought through tough physical and mental barriers on that mountain. I literally felt danger and death hovering close by. I pushed harder than I thought I could, and then I pushed more in order to continue living.

Day-to-day choices are usually not so striking, but we are all being stalked nevertheless. Life is asking what price you are willing to pay. Will you fold and negotiate away your values or take a stand for what is most important? Will you live as the most empowered version of yourself?

Personal Journaling Exercise
What different actions would the most empowered version
of me be doing?

Soul Statement Example
I am fearless love and I got this.

Inspiration From the Future You
When you know and accept yourself, fearlessness is a natural outcome. Let the future you be a source of inspiration. Hold a marathon mentality. What I mean by this is to realize that there is no finish

line and that is okay. Be the version of you that focuses on how you can improve instead of falling into defeatism.

Envision a 5 or 10-years-in-the-future you as your personal hero and know that this person exists inside you in real-time, right now. Let this knowledge help you stop practicing whatever is not really you.

Letter from Your Future Self (5 or 10 years in the future)
This is what life is like now for me...
Things that you didn't need to worry or stress over were...
I love and respect the following qualities that you have now...
Please trust and know that you will become me.
Welcome home.

Return to Inner Knowing and Sureness
Remember that every woman is radiant when inhabiting her pleasure and joy. Every man is compelling when in touch with his deep clarity and sureness. Learning to speak as informed by deeper knowing can help re-orient a conversation, an entire relationship or even a life's direction.

You don't have to sound like a complainer in order to share what's in your heart. Share your needs as a form of self-respect. Show up, pay attention and look for a way to serve. Action creates more clarity. Know thyself, then go forth and do great things.

Soul Statement Examples
The deep me is the real me.
My hero is the person I'm becoming.
I serve a higher purpose.

Perhaps the first rule of everything we endeavor to do is to pay attention. Perhaps the second is to be patient. And perhaps a third is to be attentive to what the body knows. ~ Barry Lopez

Self-realization is not for the future. Head is theory. Love is texture. Body is truth. Soul is you. Soul Statements can elevate and transform your experience of life.

You can be a more integrated and transparent communicator. You can deepen your self-care commitment and practice. You can offer yourself more fully to life. You are the one that you've been waiting for.

Prayer
May I serve life.

RESOURCES

Ronald A. Alexander, Ph.D.: *Core Creativity* (Lanham: Rowman & Littlefield, 2022)

Ronald A. Alexander, Ph.D.: *Wise Mind Open Mind* (Oakland: New Harbinger, 2009)

Catherine Auman, LMFT, *Tantric Mating* (Los Angeles: Green Tara Press, 2022)

Martha Beck: *The Way of Integrity* (New York: Penquin Life, 2021)

Kelly Bryson: *Don't Be Nice, Be Real* (Santa Rosa: Elite Books, 2004)

Benjamin Decker: *Practical Meditation for Beginners* (Althea Press, 2018)

John Dupuy: *Integral Recovery* (Albany: Excelsior Editions, 2013)

Human Awareness Institute

iAwake Technologies

Seva Kenn: *When Lovers Attack* (Sedona: Seva Media, 2019)

George Kohlrieser: *Hostage at the Table* (San Francisco: Jossey-Bass, 2006)

Bruce H. Lipton, Ph.D.: *The Biology of Belief* (Carlsbad: Hay House Inc., 2016)

Barry Lopez: *Embrace Fearlessly the Burning World* (New York: Random House, 2022)

Judith Orloff, MD: *The Empath's Survival Guide* (Boulder: Sounds True, 2018)

Judith Orloff, MD: *The Power of Surrender* (New York: Harmony, 2015)

Judith Orloff, MD: *The Power of Surrender Cards* (Carlsbad: Hay House, Inc., 2015)

Tony Robbins: *Notes From a Friend* (New York: Simon & Schuster, 1995)

Jan Robinson: *Itty Bitty Have More Sex Book* (El Segundo: Suzy Prudden, 2016)

Lorin Roche, PhD: The Radiance Sutras, (Boulder: Sounds True, 2014)

Chade-Meng Tan: *Joy On Demand* (New York: HarperOne, 2016)

John Trudell: *Bone Days* (Daemon Records, 2006)

Marianne Williamson: *The Law of Divine Compensation* (New York: Harper One, 2012)

ACKNOWLEDGMENTS

I hold deep respect for my two amazing sons, Cree and Skye.
You both changed the course of my star. I'm who I am today for
your presence, teaching and love. Thank you.

I owe much to these teachers: Bodhi Avinasha, Kelly Bryson, Scott
Catamas, Joan Gough, Charles Muir, Baba Dez Nichols, Leah Piper,
Peter Sandhill, Leong Tan and Rolling Thunder.

I'm hugely grateful to KamalaDevi McClure for coaching me through
this book-writing process. They are truly a shaman-extraordinaire
doing amazing work in the world.

Special thanks to Lisa Frechette, Tricia Holleman, Reggie Jordan,
Nina Kaiser, Jessica McKay and Sabrina Suarez. You've given me
the encouragement, advice and impetus I needed to move this book
into the world.

I'm blessed with a loving and supportive extended family:
Carol Beaudoin, Maer Blueraven, Tara & Raciel Esperanza,
Caesar Lazar Folsom, Jackie & Neal Maillet, Bree & Havel Rodriguez,
Paul Seibert, Charlotte & Joe Smith and Ruthann Smith.
I love you all.

The following people have enriched my life and informed my writing: Rich Adams, Catherine Auman, Ronald A. Alexander, Sgt. Rick Bennett, Jim Benson, Tory Blue, Steve Bollinger, Jenny Boris, Rhonda Bryant, Ann Buck, Dana Cappiello, Jim Channon, Michael Clinchy, Jeff & Ruth Coffin, Mike Daily, Heather Rae Dawn, Ben Decker, Eva Del Re, Sheryl Engelhardt, Felice Dunas, Christy Williams Dunton, John Dupuy, David Evans, L. Bradley Folsom, Susan Foxley, Cheryl Good, Catherine Greely, Warren J. Harding, Troy & Erika Harrison, David Holladay, Lindy James, Loic Jassy, Seva Kenn, Scott Kuipers, Alexsandra Marianetti, Camille Maurine, Joe McDonald, Reid Mihalko, Daryl Miller, Ora Nadrich, Liz Olsen, Judith Orloff, David Patawaran, Emily Orum, Pam Parsons, Michael Porter, Brett Prunty, Lorin Roche, Rabbi Don Singer, Jeremy Smith, Lisa Tahir, Dennis Thompson, Sykie Toles, Stephanie Torres, Karen & Larry Wells and Monte Wells.

I have great admiration for, and learn so much from, my coaching clients. Your commitment to growth and self-betterment is a constant inspiration as you move beyond obstacles and claim the life you were meant for.

ABOUT THE AUTHOR

Corey Lyon Folsom has been a professional tracker, aboriginal skills instructor, wilderness guide for newly sober people and vision quest leader. After a spiritual soul-awakening, Corey participated in the Human Awareness Institute (HAI), Source School of Tantra Yoga, Sedona School of Temple Arts, Love Coach Academy and Tony Robbins programs.

As a Certified Tantra Educator and a love & relationship coach since 2012, he assists people from all over the world to increase the soulfulness, clarity and ease with which they experience life.

Corey's committed to daily movement and frequent visits to places that nurture attunement. Corey is the father of two adult sons and he lives in California.

Contact Corey for personal coaching, interviews or speaking events.

www.CoreRelationship.com

Facebook ~ CoreF
Instagram ~ coreylyonfolsom
Discord ~ www.metamountaineers.xyz

Printed in the USA
CPSIA information can be obtained
at www.ICGtesting.com
LVHW010854021023
758327LV00043B/321